curiosity

30 Designs for Products and Interiors

Birkhäuser – Publishers for Architecture
Basel • Boston • Berlin

Frame Publishers
Amsterdam

Curiosity
30 Designs for Products
and Interiors
Frame Monographs of
Contemporary Interior
Architects

Publishers
Frame Publishers
www.framemag.com
Birkhäuser – Publishers
for Architecture
www.birkhauser.ch
Concept and design
COMA Amsterdam/New York
www.coma-web.com
Texts
Carolien van Tilburg, with
contributions by Issey
Miyake, Naoki Sakai
Copy editing
Donna de Vries-Hermansader
Translation
InOtherWords: Donna
de Vries-Hermansader
Colour reproduction
Graphic Link,
the Netherlands
Printing
Veenman drukkers,
the Netherlands

Distribution
Benelux, China, Japan,
Korea and Taiwan
ISBN 90-806445-7-9
Frame Publishers
Lijnbaansgracht 87hs
NL-1015 GZ Amsterdam
the Netherlands
www.framemag.com

All other countries
ISBN 3-7643-6743-1
Birkhäuser – Publishers
for Architecture
P.O. Box 133
CH-4010 Basel
Switzerland
Member of the Bertelsmann-
Springer Publishing Group
www.birkhauser.ch

© 2002 Frame
© 2002 Birkhäuser

A CIP catalogue record for
this book is available from
the Library of Congress,
Washington D.C., USA

Deutsche Bibliothek Cata-
loging-in-Publication Data
Curiosity / [written by
Carolien van Tilburg. Copy
ed. Donna de Vries-
Hermansader ; Billy Nolan].
Basel ; Boston ; Berlin :
Birkhäuser;

Amsterdam : Frame Publ.,
2002 (Frame monographs
of contemporary interior
architects)
ISBN 3-7643-6743-1
ISBN 90-806445-7-9

Printed on acid-free paper
produced from chlorine-
free pulp. TCF∞
Printed in the Netherlands
987654321

contents

perfect surprises

A portrait of Curiosity reads like an adventure story. Young French designer wins a trip to Japan, where he builds a career as an industrial designer and meets his Japanese partner, with whom he sets up a design agency that attracts one great client after another.

After seeing the movie *Star Wars* some 20 years ago, he set his sights on becoming a designer. In the spring of 2002, *Design News* called him one of the 11 most successful young Japanese designers. As revealed by his name, however, Gwenaël Nicolas (1966) is not Japanese, but French.

At the age of 23, the Breton graduated as an interior designer from L'Ecole Supérieure d'Arts Graphiques in Paris and, some time later, as an industrial designer from the Royal College of Art in London. In 1991 an aeroplane seat that he designed for British Airways won him a round-trip ticket to Tokyo. His initial plan was to tour the city of temples and high-tech for a fortnight. Stacks of design books on Japan had whetted his curiosity. As early as the 1980s, Japan had become a Valhalla for designers. The country was a spacious breeding ground for creativity, and extravagant projects were no exception.

Fascinated by the dynamic that is Tokyo, he decided to stay, even though his arrival had coincided more or less with the burst of Japan's bubble economy. It wasn't easy for designers to keep their heads above water in those days. Nicolas managed to find a job at an interface design studio, however. Working at Saurus provided a means of support during those first few months, a period in which he was still looking for a *sensei*, or master. 'As a designer, you need someone who makes you think, who challenges you,' he says. 'A person to look to for knowledge and information.'

In search of contacts, but unfamiliar with the Japanese language and culture, he crafted a number of tiny boxes and put a seed into each one, along with a note that said: 'Let this seed be a token of my appreciation.' He sent the little packages to people he wanted to work with: potential *sensei*. Naoki Sakai, a well-known marketeer at Waterstudio who had various popular retro-style products to his name, was intrigued by the minuscule gift.

Collaboration between Sakai and Nicolas began when the former invited the latter to participate in an exhibition on *butsudan*, the Japanese term for a mini altar found in nearly every Japanese household: a small shrine honouring the family dead. While other participants – a select company of architects and designers – had expressed themselves through highly extraordinary designs, Nicolas's contribution was remarkable for its elegant simplicity. A few months later, his miniature temple was the only *butsudan* from the exhibition that had actually gone into production.

This baptism of fire was followed by one joint project after another. Together, Nicolas and Sakai have come up with everything from futuris-

'Sakai's advice was, "Never try to change technical specifications.
Change just one thing in the design. Usually that's enough.
Products evolve – you're not going to spark an overnight revolution."'

tic telephones, stereo equipment and cameras to railway-car interiors and a sofa for Cassina Inter Décor. And as both men are itching to merge their talents in the design and realisation of a car, surely the world hasn't seen the last of their collaborative efforts.

Nicolas has learned everything from his *sensei* except design. As a specialist in presentation and communication, Sakai has concentrated on teaching him the ins and outs of Japanese business. He leaves the design aspect of a project completely to Nicolas. 'Sakai never tinkers with my design. He trusts me implicitly. He takes a considerable risk every time we work together, because sometimes I don't have a definitive design until the presentation is imminent and it's too late to make any changes. Obviously, Sakai likes surprises – not only for himself, but also for the client.'

According to Nicolas, Sakai is ahead of his time. His products are especially successful in niche markets. Rather than taking a specific design or technique as his point of departure, he imagines himself as the consumer and asks: What am I looking for in a product? In the early '80s, for example, Sakai suggested giving all those angular compact cars a rounder, friendlier silhouette. His recommendation led to Nissan's Be-1 and Pao models. Working with Olympus at that time, he launched the firm's O.Product, an aluminium camera with an angular look that *did* get Sakai's seal of approval.

Recalling those days, Nicolas says, 'Sakai's advice was, "Never try to change technical specifications. Change just one thing in the design. Usually that's enough. Products evolve – you're not going to spark an overnight revolution."' But the emphasis on technology began to annoy Nicolas at that time. 'The Japanese electronics industry is obsessed with the launch of new models and has little interest in design. In most cases, design is an extension of engineering.' Discussing the subject in 2002, Nicolas detects a change in Japanese views on product design and the importance of technology. He sees no-nonsense products like the Muji CD player designed by Naoto Fukasawa (IDEO Japan) as the first signs of this reversal.

After four years spent primarily in the field of product design, Gwenaël was ready to expand his frontiers. 'I felt as though my clients no longer had a great deal to teach me.' A review of events in the rest of the design world brought him to fashion designer Issey Miyake, whose uniquely displayed retail collections made a big impression on Nicolas. 'Although the shops seem empty, they're filled with a tremendous sense of tension. I wanted to discover his secret.' After countless visits to Miyake's Aoyama boutique, a space whose ingenious fabrics and minimal interior design never failed to absorb his attention, Nicolas decided to do something that would make Miyake notice him.

Aware that the fashion designer receives numerous portfolios from young designers on a daily basis, Nicolas added a concept for a fashion show to the portfolio containing his projects. 'It's essential to make a connection with the person you're trying to impress,' he says. 'If I'd sent him my portfolio of telephone designs, I doubt that he'd have spotted a link between him and me.' Nicolas submitted a maquette of an inflatable treadmill that would allow models to walk on water, as it were, while showing the latest collection. Miyake contacted him the very same day, and within twenty-four hours Nicolas was face to face with his design idol. To his great surprise, what had caught Miyake's eye was the Frenchman's very first product: the *butsudan*. As for the fashion show on water, Miyake said it wouldn't work.

Another surprise came when, at the same meeting, Miyake gave him a week to come up with a retail design for a shop in Paris. With no real experience in this field, Nicolas sketched five interiors, one of which Miyake selected and subsequently realised. Apparently Nicolas had made his mark, as demonstrated by the commissions that followed: retail interiors in Tokyo, New York and, again, Paris.

These shops accommodate the fashion designer's Pleats Please brand. Simple, no-frills interiors that reflect the atmosphere found in other Miyake outlets, they feature bold accents: attention-getters that nearly always have a practical purpose as well. Nicolas minimises the visible functions of a space by combining storage and display, for example. In Paris, panels above the garments become a video screen after dark. The huge green cube that Nicolas suspended in the New York shop includes a counter. In another Paris shop, a honeycomb 'sculpture' serves as both focal point and display unit, and a cool blue cube lends access to the fitting rooms. A brightly coloured curtain in the Tokyo outlet conceals both fitting rooms and storeroom.

For Miyake's 'me' label, on the other hand, Nicolas designed a colourless shop based entirely on a transparent display-and-storage system. Visible inside see-through packaging tubes, the apparel for sale forms the only chromatic accent. The interior is a prime example of efficiently used space. A distinct division of disciplines is no longer apparent. In Nicolas's total design, which includes packaging, storage space, graphics and interior.

In 1998, with seven or so adventurous years in Tokyo behind him, Nicolas teamed up with marketeer Reiko Miyamoto and went into business as Curiosity. Their design studio is located on a narrow shopping street in what looks like an ordinary neighbourhood, but one glimpse of the nearby skyscrapers of Shinjuku brings with it the realisation that this is the heart of Tokyo. The ground-floor space that functions as both gallery and conference room is regularly transformed into a mock-up of the latest interior-design project. The sober, white room upstairs accommodates a row of six designers in deep concentration. 'At the moment, Curiosity is primarily Gwenaël,' says Miyamoto, 'but I think that in a couple of years our other creative designers will be assuming more and more responsibility.'

Prototypes and models are scattered throughout the space. The conference area – two Boomerang sofas and a coffee table – is squeezed between office and kitchen. With six years of marketing experience at ad agency Daiko, Miyamoto is the firm's chief planner and marketeer. She's active in the concept phase of product-design projects, in which she focuses on what the consumer wants. Miyamoto seems to be fulfilling the same role as Sakai once did, although unlike him, she's also involved in the design process.

The pragmatic Miyamoto is an analytical coach for Nicolas, who loves to assemble the jigsaw puzzle that leads to the ultimate design. 'Reiko is my harshest critic,' he laughs. 'But quite often she gets me going on the right track, and I have complete faith in her marketing instincts.' In the case of interior designs, she does the planning and carries out research to find suitable materials. Although their preference for simplicity

and elegance stands out, the results of their work are more than merely beautiful. There is inevitably an extra dimension to the product and its functional aspect. The Le Feu d'Issey atomiser, for instance, appears only when the user lifts the little ball. Sakai put it aptly when he called this extra dimension 'design in action'. Miyamoto refers to the phenomenon as 'discovery'.

Backed by experience as a product designer, Nicolas knows as no other that between drawing board and production lies a highly instructive phase: the construction of a prototype. He uses the complicated full-size contraptions in his studio as guinea pigs, so to speak. At first glance everything looks set to go, but gaping tool boxes and a snarl of cables in one corner show that the operation is poised in midstream. A prototype of an interior is, for that matter, an exception to the rule in Japan. Designers here seldom have time for prototypes. The country's sky-high rents force retailers to open their doors as quickly as

possible. An example is the Pleats Please shop in Aoyama, a race-against-the-clock project for which Nicolas had only 30 days from design to opening. 'In a case like that,' he says, 'the designer is primarily a decision maker.' His decisions were aimed at time, money and quality.

Nicolas sees retail design as an extension of product design. 'I approach an interior as though it were a product. Every outside has an inside. And the space should be attractive from both positions. I try to imagine the effect that light, volume and materials will have on the space in question. I look for a focal point, and I concentrate on motion, a vital ingredient of retail design. In the beginning my designs were rather static, but now I try to create a flow of spontaneous movement through the space. A shop should be more than a feast for the eyes. If you don't move, you don't see the product. Furthermore, people should be able to look at the merchandise from different perspectives. What I do now is play with the combination

'A shop should be more than a feast for the eyes. If you don't move, you don't see the product'

of impact, flow and a graphically photogenic result. The graphic aspect of a shop creates a long-lasting image in people's minds.'

His work doesn't end there. A close look at Curiosity's interiors reveals an extraordinary attention to detail. Nothing is left to chance. Take the Tag Heuer shops, for example, which illustrate an interesting transition from interior design to product design. The first impression is a space that seems cold and aloof, somewhat shocking. 'The shop almost hurts,' Nicolas remarks with satisfaction. The Tokyo outlet, in particular, required craftsmen to examine and mull over every square millimetre of space. In this shop, transparent cubes used for displaying exclusive watches revolve 90 degrees while keeping the small trays they contain horizontal – a gentle rocking back and forth is barely noticeable. Another fine detail is the lock, which is visible only for the moment it takes to remove a watch from the cube. Such refinements are discovered, however, only by those willing to slow their pace and take the 'time' necessary to inspect their surroundings.

A keen interest in focal points and fine details didn't save Curiosity, however, from an unfortunate experience linked to the retail design for Takeo Kikuchi. A bold red ceiling, initially meant to lead the eye momentarily up and away from the fashions, failed to create the desired effect. Only in retrospect did Nicolas realise that the plethora of clothing and accessories on display completely changed the retail environment. Having followed the approach that was so successful in the Issey Miyake boutiques, where his focus was on *one* fashion line belonging to *one* collection, Nicolas now found his highlights for the Kikuchi shop virtually overwhelmed by the merchandise.

With that negative experience in mind, when Curiosity was asked to create a standard retail design for more than 200 Dockers outlets throughout Asia, Nicolas and his team set out in a new direction. The challenge was to design an inexpensive but unique interior. The amount of money that Dockers was prepared to spend per square metre was only a tenth of what Tag Heuer had set aside for the same amount of retail space. Dockers has an extensive collection. Basing his concept on the strictly systemised organisation of the clothing brand, Nicolas designed a fixed modular interior meant to neutralise the cacophony of garments on display. Although a bit of flexibility is not out of the question, the basic elements of the layout are literally riveted to floor and ceiling, thus preserving the balance of the original design. Rather than opting for the obvious – a bright and cheery atmosphere – Nicolas created an uncluttered interior that expresses the fine quality of the casual fashions sold here. The result is a clean and surprisingly ingenious space.

Nicolas is into non-figurative design. 'I'm always trying to create something original. It doesn't have to look like anything else. I see the same kind of vision in the work of Steve Jobs. He takes Apple to a new level, time after time. The latest model isn't just an adaptation of its predecessor, but a genuine step forward.' Nicolas's restyling of the second Nintendo Game Boy, which he made into a simple toy with the look of luxury, is also based on a desire for originality.

In his ongoing search for the perfect form, Nicolas welcomes any and all ideas. Some of his more clever solutions, however, are rooted in utter simplicity. 'A rounded object, like the one I designed for Le Feu d'Issey, was so obvious that I couldn't believe it wasn't already on the market. The same thing applies to the 'me' tubes. The idea is so simple that my first thought was: Doesn't this already exist?' Nicolas's designs are never 'just for a laugh'. Everything has a function. Every design is definitive. But a design that looks spare and angular at first glance always has an underlying touch of playfulness and surprise, even though it doesn't tickle the funny bone.

Curiosity tries hard not to be repetitive. Tokyo keeps these designers on their toes. 'The city is a hub, a centre of

information. And because it's such a maelstrom of activity, it makes you want to jump in, do your thing and move on to the next level. In lots of other cities, you absorb everything around you and then grind to a halt. You don't do anything with the experience. You hoard it. That's simply not possible here. In Tokyo you have to jettison the ballast. A great feeling.'

The people at Curiosity are eager to be part of design in all its guises. But whatever the discipline, their work invariably bears a distinct signature characterised by concealment and discovery. The Lucky Goldstar portable cassette and CD player, for instance, integrates charger and speakers in one unit. It's not surprising to hear that Curiosity dreams of designing a shop for the De Beers diamond dynasty. A client entering the shop would no doubt look in vain for the glistening jewels, which would be safely ensconced, under lock and key, in discreetly placed displays. Curiosity also amazes its admirers with optical illusion and material manoeu-

vres. Although angular, the Spider sofa is unexpectedly comfy. The Spoutnik stool looks light, feels heavy. Glass display panels at Tag Heuer are surprisingly high and thick, and a perfume bottle designed for travel weighs a bit more than the one at home on the dressing table. When Curiosity explains its oddball decisions, the arguments are always sound and original.

Astrid Klein, who runs an architecture firm in Tokyo with partner Mark Dytham, calls Nicolas a 'meticulous perfectionist'. In her words: 'There is never, ever a hint of chaos or error. All his products and interiors are really finished. Nothing is left to chance or coincidence.' She has to admit, however that she doesn't find much humour in his work.

Noriko Kawakami, a design critic who writes for a number of publications, including the Japanese magazine *Axis*, praises Nicolas's versatility. 'Nobody can give a space two faces like he can. Modern and conservative. What's more, it's almost impossible to find designers in Japan that do both product design and interior design. In his attention to detail, you see the signature of the product designer.' According to Kawakami, Nicolas is one of the few young designers who has succeeded in realising retail interiors as well as products. What she finds particularly remarkable is that Nicolas, an outsider, has managed to make a place for himself in Japan, where nearly every product designer is on the staff of one of the major electronics corporations.

Looking back at *Star Wars*, his initial source of inspiration and the reason he entered the design profession, Nicolas says: 'My dream was to convert the imaginary world of the silver screen into reality. It's so easy to design spectacular things. The real challenge lies in getting your ideas realised and in making sure that people actually buy and use them.'

Vending machines are a Japanese obsession. If it exists, it's probably available in a Japanese vending machine. Everything imaginable, from soft drinks and instant noodles to train tickets and magazines – not to mention live beetles and worn knickers – is stocked in one of the country's 5.6 million automated dispensers.

Having toyed for years with the idea of a vending machine for clothing, Gwenaël Nicolas took one look at Issey Miyake's new fashion statement, 'me', and saw his chance. Thanks to an extremely elastic fabric, the brightly coloured tops have one thing in common: one size fits all. In an attempt to fully integrate space, product and packaging, Nicolas opted for a reversal of the standard design process or, in his own words, for a 'complete reset'. He started with the packaging, went on to design a dispenser and wrapped the results in a minimal spatial design. Following a presentation featuring plastic Evian bottles modified to demonstrate his concept, Nicolas was given the green light.

In the Matsuya department store in Ginza (Tokyo), a diminutive shop-in-a-shop less than 20 metres square features a Perspex wall that looks like an oversize vending machine. It contains Miyake's 'me' fashions, which are prepackaged in see-through plastic (PET) tubes with large screw tops bearing embossed, transparent logos. Removing the top takes an eternity – a deliberate stratagem, according to Nicolas, intended to emphasise a sense of exclusivity.

A diagonally positioned rack holds sample tops, which the client can try on in a fold-out fitting cubicle. Folded, the cubicle accommodates no one, but when you push together the two doors that fit over each other, the result is a pentagonal chamber with just enough room for one customer. A godsend in tight spaces.

After making her choice, the customer removes a tube from the transparent wall, and the remaining tops automatically drop into place without tumbling out of the machine. Ultra-bright lighting has a dazzling effect on the fluorescent details of the clothing. A small recess in the round counter keeps the tube from rolling away while the customer pays for her purchase. In this compact shop, every square centimetre counts.

'me'
issey miyake

The day after his first meeting with Gwenaël Nicolas, Issey Miyake asked his young acquaintance to design the interior of a shop in Paris. Heightening the tension of his first confrontation with retail design was the presence of Nicolas's former school, a building only a stone's throw away from the shop. Intent on making a good impression, just one week later Nicolas used a five-storey model to present the same number of proposals. When Miyake saw the tower, he jokingly remarked that he might have to lease every floor at the Boulevard St. Germain address. Still very green, Nicolas took the fashion designer's comment seriously. What a terrific idea!

Miyake opted for the simplest, and thus perhaps strongest, plan: a retail space that becomes a theatre for passers-by during the evening hours. By day, the Pleats Please collection is neatly displayed throughout the space, and a glance at the long acrylic wall unit – which holds neatly rolled-up items from the Pleats Please collection – reveals the palette of the season. Nicolas wanted to evoke the sense of a Japanese stationer's shop, bursting with colours and textures in every drawer and cubbyhole. Three revolving panels, centrally positioned, serve as partitions. Clothing hangs beneath these panels. At closing time, they shift to form a diagonal element that transforms the shop into a small theatre. Artistic projections of various fashions from the latest collection appear on the panels, but the clothes themselves are invisible.

Waiting for the traffic light to change at the corner of Boulevard St. Germain is far more fun at night, when the Miyake theatre is in full swing.

pleats please
st. germain

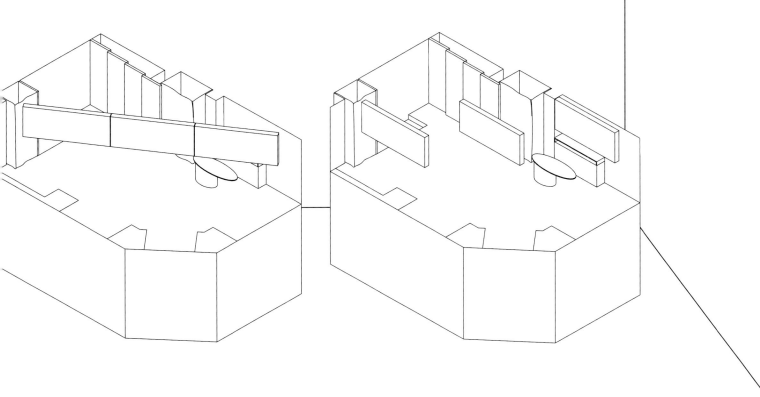

When the owner of Cassina Inter Décor Japan, an up-market furniture store, asked Nicolas for a sofa that would appeal to young people, he based his design on movement. Although the piece is officially known as Boomerang, he dubbed the design 'my first sofa', a reference to the importance of this major purchase in a young couple's life. It had to be affordable and easy to move from one dwelling to another – strong enough to survive at least two such removals – and it had to exemplify good design. With these requirements in mind, Nicolas set out to bridge the gap between his new creation and the exclusive designs that characterise much of the Cassina collection.

The result is a light-hearted yet simple design, a seating element both jaunty and solid. Slightly raised corners soften the spare lines of a sofa that wraps around you, as it were. A side view evokes the image of a boomerang: a curved shape in which Nicolas also sees a 'flying sofa'. He originally considered making the legs out of transparent acrylic, but after a lengthy search for sturdy yet affordable acrylic, he opted instead for steel legs finished in aluminium. The light, slender form is a striking contrast to the sturdy material he selected to complete the design. The seat is not soft and pliant, the fabric neither plush nor velvety, but the level of comfort is remarkable. The designer got the idea for the honeycomb surface after spotting a similar car-seat fabric in a Honda showroom.

Nicolas also developed a Boomerang bench for Cassina, a design intended for museums. A number of these benches placed side by side makes a powerful impression. The lively rhythm thus generated suggests a wave-like motion. Boomerang is available in white, blue and black.

boomerang

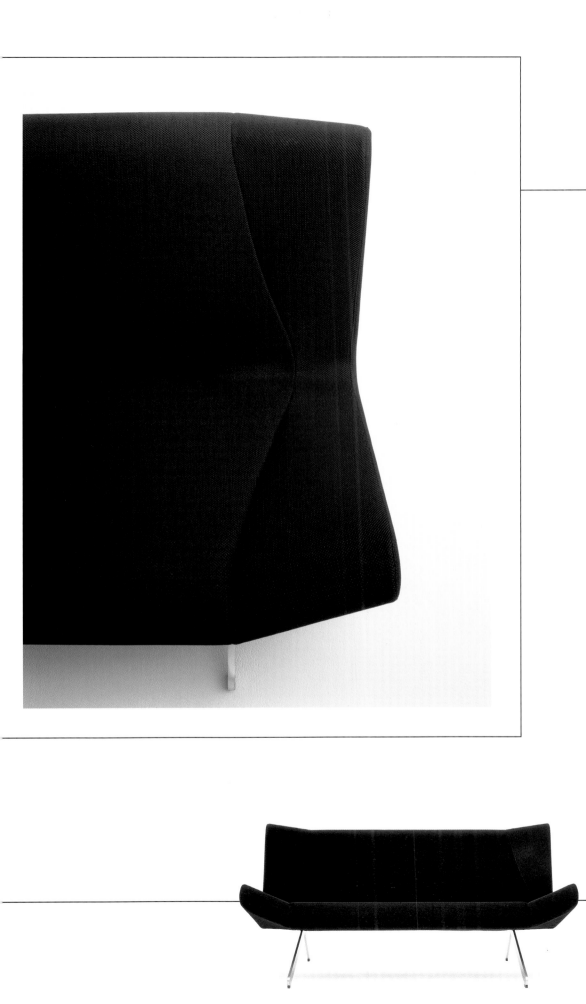

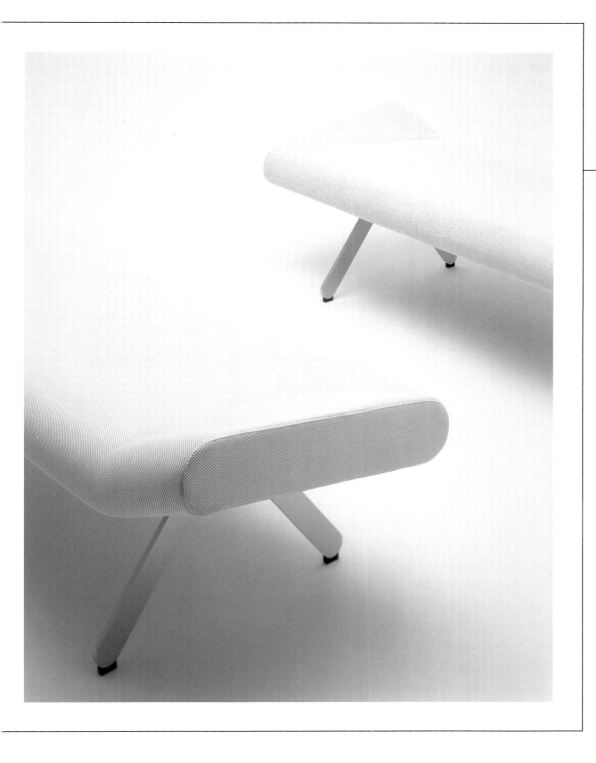

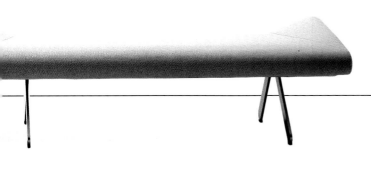

In planning the Tag Heuer façade on Omotesando, Tokyo's only real strut-your-stuff street and Japan's nod to the Champs Elysées, the French-born designer opted for a graphic look. Two oblique rectangles that appeared in his sketchbook again and again ultimately formed the basis of the design. A 4-metre-high glazed shop front offers an interior view of several cubes and two oversized, semitransparent blue glass walls adjacent to stairs that take customers to the upper floor. The introduction of blue to Tag Heuer's red-and-green logo was Nicolas's answer to the client's desire for innovation, as well as a reference to the watchmaker's nautical image.

Because the client wanted the shop to reflect the exclusive yet sporty character of the watches on display – a feature aimed at both men and women – Gwenaël Nicolas incorporated the distinguishing features of the product into the interior. In an attempt to slow the pace, he designed a simple space that invites customers to zoom in on the charm of the items on display.

A stroll through the shop reveals the soul of a designer who loves subtle details. The showcase cubes provide a good example. Although they move, the rocking motion of the trays of watches inside is so slight that the products remain perfectly horizontal. Another fine detail is the lock, which is visible only for the moment it takes to remove a watch from the cube. And openings in a glass wall covered in black film reveal intriguing glimpses of a group of watches positioned on a turntable (featuring semi-opaque film) behind the wall.

An air of aloofness rises from the silvery mat floor to complement the chic ambience created by the smooth curve of a classic walnut wall. Nicolas sees the line of a woman's body or the bow of a ship in the curve of this wall – a warm surface that noticeably lowers the chill factor in the shop. The choice of inexpensive but durable flooring allowed Nicolas to realise spectacular custom-designed display cases and other interesting methods of product presentation within the agreed budget. He solved the problem of a low ceiling by strictly limiting the amount of overhead light. This gives the visitor one less reference point, thus creating the illusion of extra height.

At the rear of the shop a glass partition covered in blue film subtly separates the VIP lounge – a space both solitary and chic – from the rest of the shop.

Similarly designed outlets have opened recently in London, New York and Kuala Lumpur.

tag heuer
tokyo

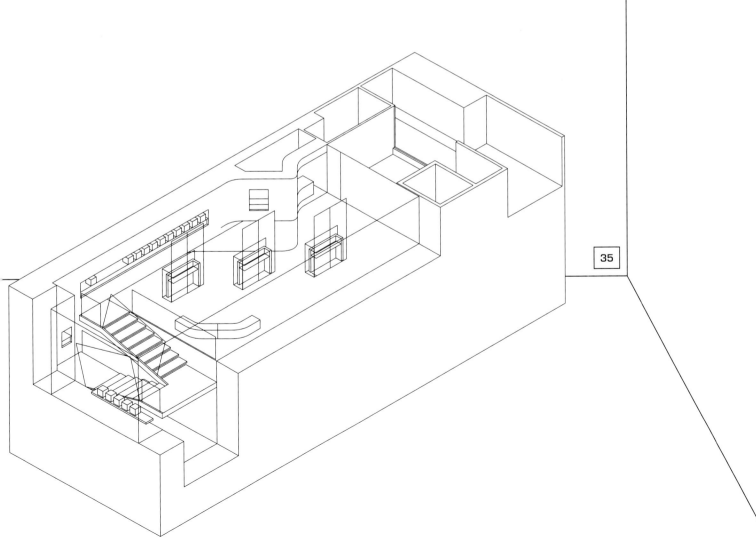

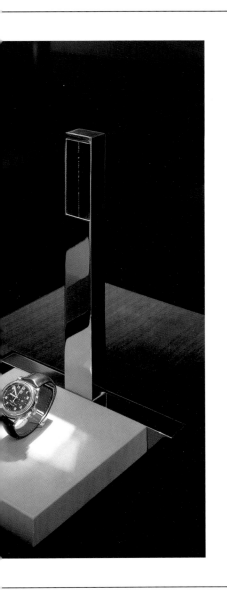

With no prior knowledge of the *butsudan*, a miniature Buddhist temple kept in Japanese homes to honour the dead, Nicolas accepted Naoki Sakai's request to design an extraordinary example for a butsudan exhibition. The brief gave contributors carte blanche. Not even art installations were taboo; the designs would never be commercial products anyway. Other participants included the renowned architects Shigeru Uchida, Alan Chang and Kisho Kurokawa. The event was not a competition but a brainstorming session. Nicolas wasn't interested in making something weird, however. He envisioned a temple that radiated quality, an object of obvious value. He further challenged himself to create a design that could be mass produced.

He remembered seeing an exclusive wooden box at his brother's house. Nothing on the exterior revealed the contents: an expensive bottle of whisky. Nicolas based his design on the charisma of that simple box. Taking a tautly linear wooden cube as his point of departure, he provided the front with subtly rounded forms for a modern, elegant touch. Hinges suggest a receptacle, complete with contents. When the doors are opened, the rounded forms disappear, leaving angular structures in their wake.

Nicolas wanted an interior with the kind of complex structure so characteristic of Japanese temples, but he failed to find what he was looking for in Japanese architecture books. Ultimately, he based the interior on complicated constructions from early 20th-century Russian architecture. Sensing the importance of making an object to please not only the human eye but also a greater eye capable of observing the temple as a whole, he tinkered for countless hours before finding the structure he wanted. His goal was a miniature temple with depth. 'The deeper you look inside,' he says, 'the older things become. I wanted it to represent a journey into the past.' And like a full-size temple, the butsudan was to be a serene balance of tranquillity and complexity.

A rare exception among many exuberant and fanciful contributions to the exhibition, Nicolas's butsudan immediately grabbed the attention of a manufacturer. A minor triumph for the Frenchman, for whom a traditional Japanese object became the first of his designs to actually go into production. His prototype drew virtually no criticism. The only thing added was the little drawer-cum-table needed to accommodate incense and ancestral photographs.

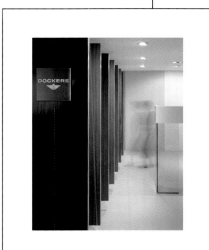

In Namba, a massive underground shopping mall in the heart of Osaka, the entrance to the Takeo Kikuchi boutique is a nearly open façade. Openness aside, however, flanking black walls and low-key lighting pose a barrier. In dividing up the large space, Curiosity was determined to create an interior that would automatically direct the focus of the eye and, consequently, the movement through the shop. A gigantic red box suspended from the ceiling screens the front part of the boutique. This 'mask' is precisely what Gwenaël Nicolas had in mind. By drawing attention to the ceiling, he has managed to lure the observer into the central area of the underground shop. 'People look up at the ceiling, see a "reverse museum" and feel refreshed,' is his rather cryptic explanation.

Small openings in a white wall offer a peek at fire-engine-red showcases. Peering through these spyholes, customers spot little metal ladders and video graphics. This area offers an abundance of accessories, and visitors are encouraged to take a closer look at everything in sight.

At the rear of the space, a deep-pile red carpet forms a striking contrast to the simple wooden floor seen in the rest of the shop. Seated on the Spider sofa designed by Curiosity and surrounded by a suspended stainless-steel grille, customers try on exclusive Takeo Kikuchi footwear. An outlet like this one provides them with a comprehensive 'head, shoulders, knees and toes' experience. A rather fanciful design is the ingenious shelving system for suits and accessories, which features a lazy Susan tie display.

During the opening the client, a big cycling fan, couldn't take his eyes off his favourite merchandise, a handsome display of bicycles. Today's assortment no longer features twin-wheeled transport, however. Along with clothing and footwear, customers now find a wide variety of gadgets and other 'must-haves' at Takeo Kikuchi.

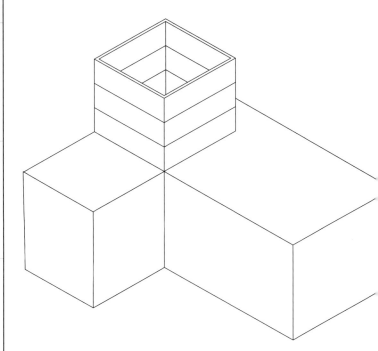

The designer began by analysing a number of basic assumptions. Why use standard packaging if the product can be presented in a new way? Does the base of a bottle of essence oil have to be flat? Why do shower-gel products nearly always have caps with oval indentations? Is it really necessary for a viscous substance to be in a tube that flares at the closed end? Without effecting an appreciable difference in cost, Nicolas provided exclusive packaging for the whole new essence-based line. Tubes stand upright, caps are relatively flat, and the shampoo bottle is strikingly tall and narrow. The look is cool and lucid, despite asymmetric graphics on the bottles that play tricks with an otherwise evenly balanced design. Twelve products vary from a basic oil to bath and skincare products, and even include a necklace. Shaped like the cap that tops the bottle of essence oil, the pendant on a chain is made of a fluid-absorbing metal.

Nicolas is in complete charge of the product launch. The box holding the basic oil boasts an extra wrapper and a lid. The unique packaging accentuates the trademark and requires a bit of extra effort – just the touch needed to enhance the desired aura of luxury. A terrific gift for the sophisticated Japanese consumer who finds the envelope fully as meaningful as the message itself.

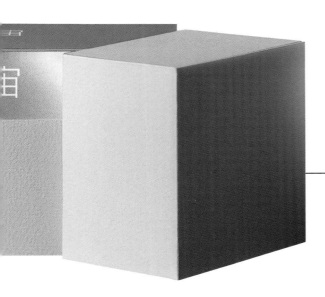

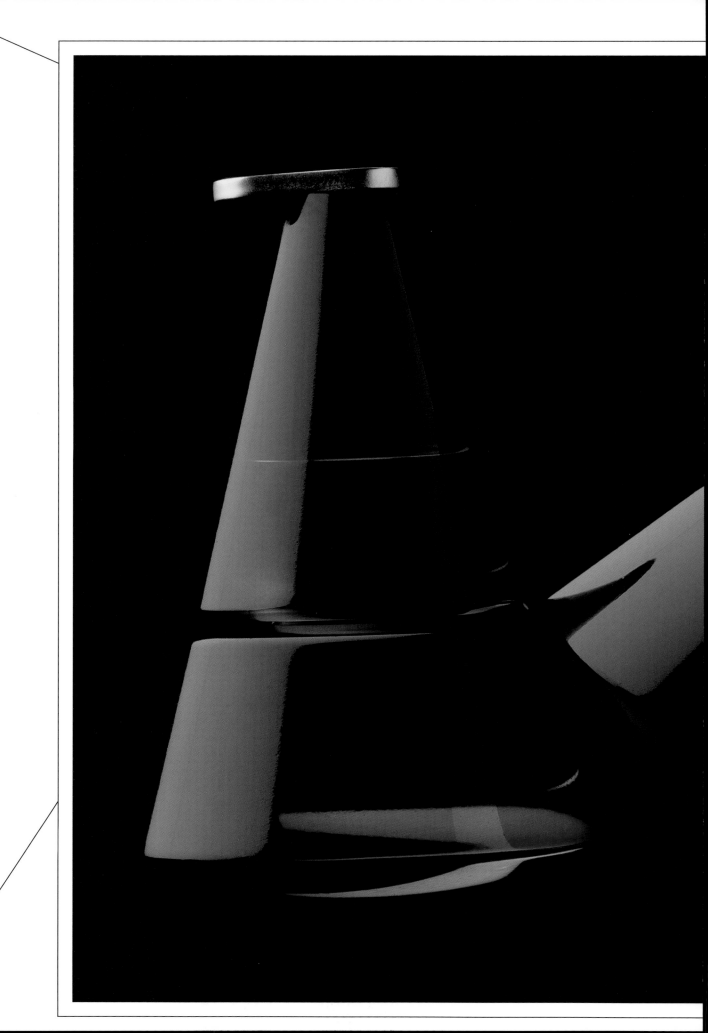

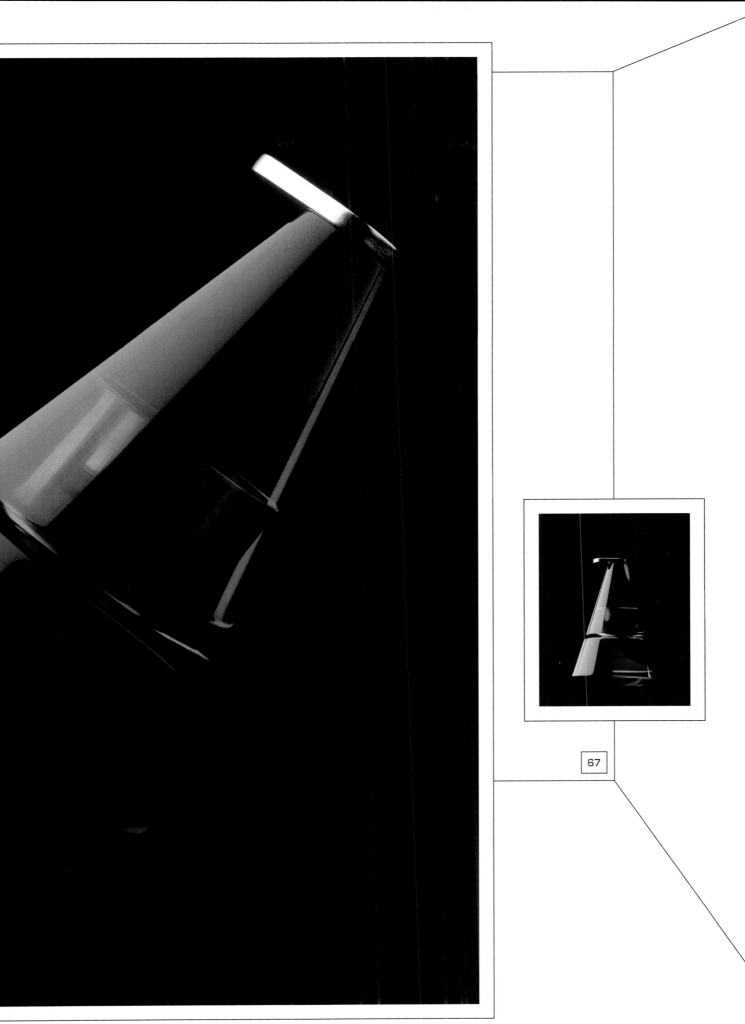

One might think that a product designer asked to create the packaging for a travel-size scent bottle would focus on two qualities: lightweight and convenient. Not Nicolas. He dismissed the whole idea of a travel-size bottle for Zanzibar – Van Cleef & Arpels' fragrance for men – in favour of his own concept: a masculine object radiating a sense of value. Nicolas wanted a bottle that, even when nearly empty, would go straight into the suitcase and not into the wastepaper basket.

Thinking in terms of something weighty, angular and hard, he came up with a flat bottle packaged in a square metal container, which feels unusually heavy for a scent bottle. His maxim was 'the heavier, the better'. The idea of fragrance as ornament was, according to Nicolas, a fitting characterisation of a product manufactured by Van Cleef & Arpels, a company with a long-standing reputation as jewellery makers. Marketing research confirmed the designer's opinion, moreover, that men see quality in a product that carries a bit of weight.

The empty glass bottle can be replaced by a refill inserted from below. A diagonally positioned, slightly protruding atomiser adds an element of tension to the simple design, while a recess beneath the atomiser offers a view of the red glass bottle and its contents. The colour red refers to the original Zanzibar packaging, with its lozenge-shaped red cap. It goes without saying that the new design does not have a separate cap, as Nicolas dislikes interrupting the form of an object by adding functional components such as this. A prime example is the continuous shape of his design for Le Feu d'Issey.

Thanks to an exterior container made of aluminium, a relatively light material, the definitive product is not terribly heavy. To be on the safe side, in launching the new design Van Cleef & Arpels downplayed the notion of a travel-size bottle and accentuated the use of this 'metal atomiser'.

Nonetheless, Nicolas was successful in convincing his client of the advantages of a hefty packaging style and an object that a man will take with him rather than discard in a hotel room far from home.

aqua pleats

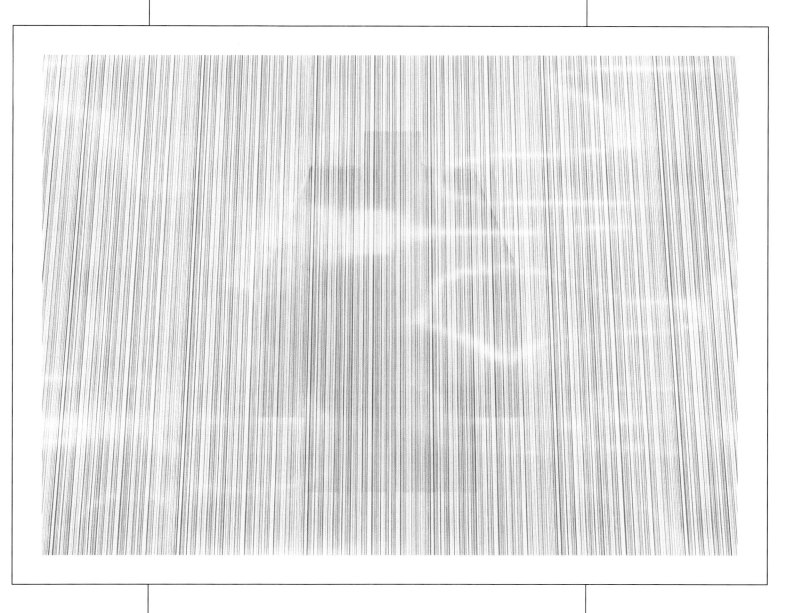

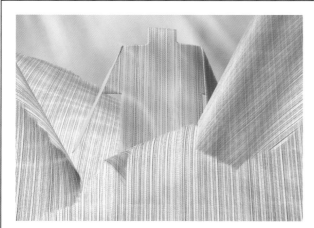  

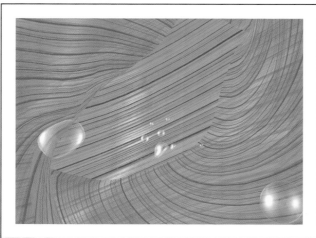 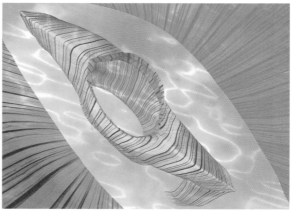 

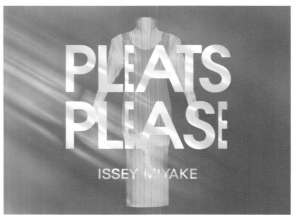

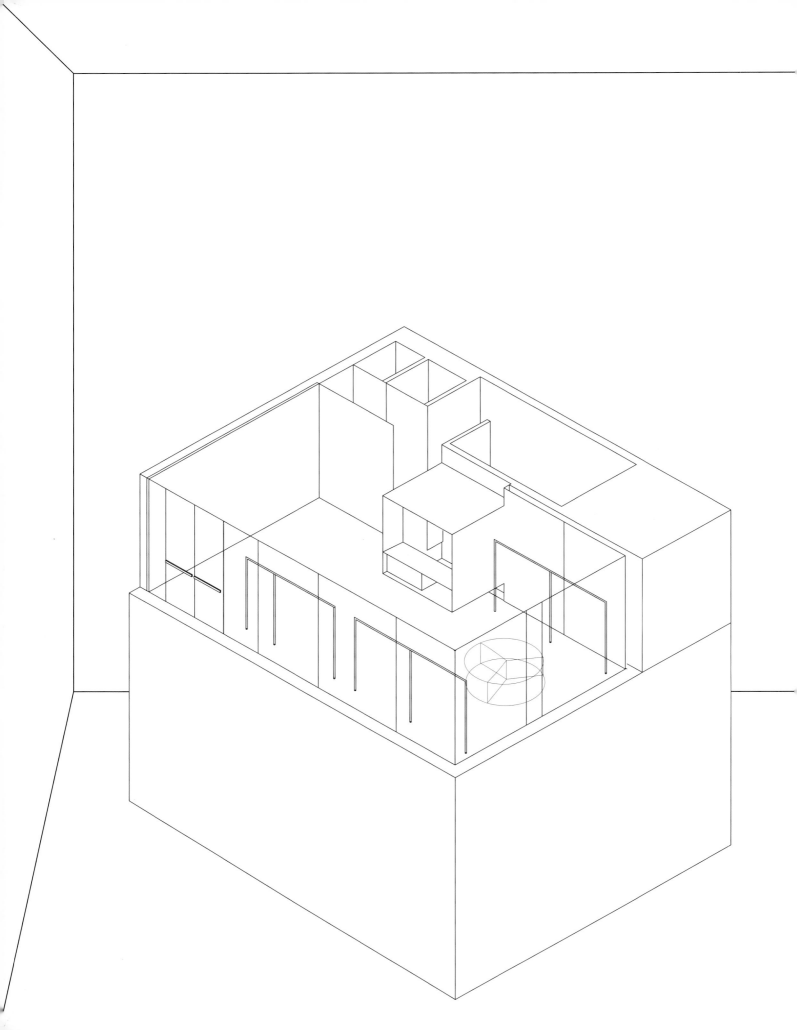

pleats please new york

When Nicolas first showed Issey Miyake his concept for
the Pleats Please shop in New York, the fashion designer
thought it was a joke. The concept featured a gigantic
green cube, and green is definitely not Miyake's favourite
colour. He thinks the colour clashes with most skin tones
and that people wearing green look unhealthy. Nicolas
chose green as a contrast to the terracotta tint of the
façade. He found red and yellow a boring duo and red and
blue too dark. Furthermore, Nicolas wondered if green
would really prove to be the wrong colour for a clothing
store. In this particular case, Miyake can draw a sigh of
relief, as customers are arriving at the shop in droves.
Those passing the boutique at the corner of Prince Street
become inquisitive when it's not immediately apparent
what's going on behind the scenes. The establishment has
no ordinary shop window. A big glass box inside – covered
with Lumisty film, which is transparent only when you
stand right in front of it – contains the retail space.

Major difficulties slowed down the construction phase.
At the outset of the renovation, the basic structure of the
200-year-old building, literally on the verge of collapse, had
to be restored. Steel panels now hold the wall in place, and
the film-covered glass further blocks the view of the wall.
Thanks to these interventions, customers have no sense
of being in an old building. At the core of the shop, a metal
frame supports the suspended green cube, which is an
icon of what SoHo once was: a hub of avant-garde galleries
and visual art.

spoutnik

One of the many projects that Nicolas has done for Issey Miyake is the design of a small stool for a compact fitting room. He opted for a transparent acrylic seat to make the stool appear as small as possible. The seat perched on three slender legs may look fragile, but in fact the thick acrylic used for this stool can carry a lot of weight, and its stainless-steel base is as solid as a rock. A round stainless-steel plate at the centre of the seat is actually the head of a large screw that fastens seat and legs together. The screw makes the object easy to dismantle and transport, and also comes in handy when a damaged acrylic seat needs to be replaced. The name of the object is rooted in its antenna-like appearance, which reminds Nicolas of early artificial satellites.

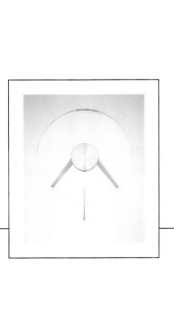

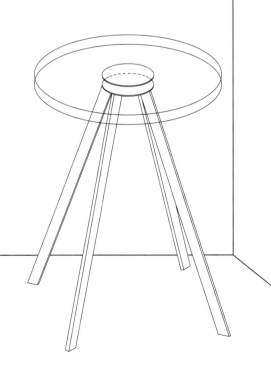

The first time he met with Gwenaël Nicolas to discuss his new fragrance, Le Feu d'Issey, fashion designer Issey Miyake unwittingly indicated the shape of the bottle. To show that he wanted something that would feel good to hold, he curled his fingers around an imaginary ball. Nicolas eventually packaged the bottle in a translucent sphere made of red plastic. The colour is a direct reference to *le feu* ('fire'), and the material reinforces the message, as plastic is never cold to the touch. The globular shape was so obvious that Nicolas researched his choice to make sure he wasn't copying an existing idea.

In a technical sense, the apparently simple product proved to be more complex than it looks. It took a lot of brainwork before the engineers found the right balance of rigidity and translucency. Both prototypes were launched, one as a basic container and the other as a travel version.

Another of Nicolas's goals was a scent bottle without a removable cap. The bottle was to have a 'total look', whether in use or simply waiting to be picked up. Nicolas shivers at the unsightly nightmare of dozens of topless scent bottles standing half naked on counters in department stores and airports. His ingenious solution was to conceal the atomiser inside the container. The spray mechanism in the basic container appears only after the user picks up the ball, while the atomiser belonging to the travel version can be removed from the rubber sphere with a simple twist and subsequently clicked into position behind several minuscule rubber balls.

Nicolas also designed the bath line, which features bright shades of orange, yellow and green.

pioneer audio

Electronics giant Pioneer asked Naoki Sakai of Waterstudio to come up with some creative designs for stereo equipment. Sakai, in turn, called on Nicolas. At the time, most equipment of this sort boasted an excess of buttons, knobs and functions. Nicolas set out to minimise what he saw as zillions of useless functions. His goal was a simple but stylish stereo system. Inspired by the work of Taniguchi, the architect commissioned to design the new Museum of Modern Art in New York, Nicolas concentrated on purity of line and the concept of floating glass.

Attached to twin speakers with a click are stereo modules, which span the two 'piers' like a glass bridge. Between glazed front and hardware-containing cabinet is a gap of less than a centimetre. An aluminium frame connects the two components: one glass, one metal.

Seiko had recently developed a watch with an LCD function featuring white graphics that seemed to float in the glass dial. Spare, futuristic and minimal. Nicolas studied the watchmaker's technology and developed a new interface. Visible in the glass front of his design for Pioneer is a 'floating image' that conveys information relevant to the stereo equipment. A thin layer of film on the glass serves as a touchscreen, which is linked to highly sensitive metal wires in the glass and, subsequently, to the electronic equipment.

An easy-to-use design was high on Nicolas's list of priorities. By simply turning the round knob on the remote control, the user regulates the volume. He can switch to another function by touching the front of the CD player, for example, or pressing the corresponding icon on the remote control.

After reviewing the design, Pioneer was interested primarily in the use of frosted glass as a material for a stereo set. Little else remains to be seen in the manufacturer's definitive product. Glass was spotted as a source of inspiration for other brands as well, who soon began marketing stereo equipment with glass components.

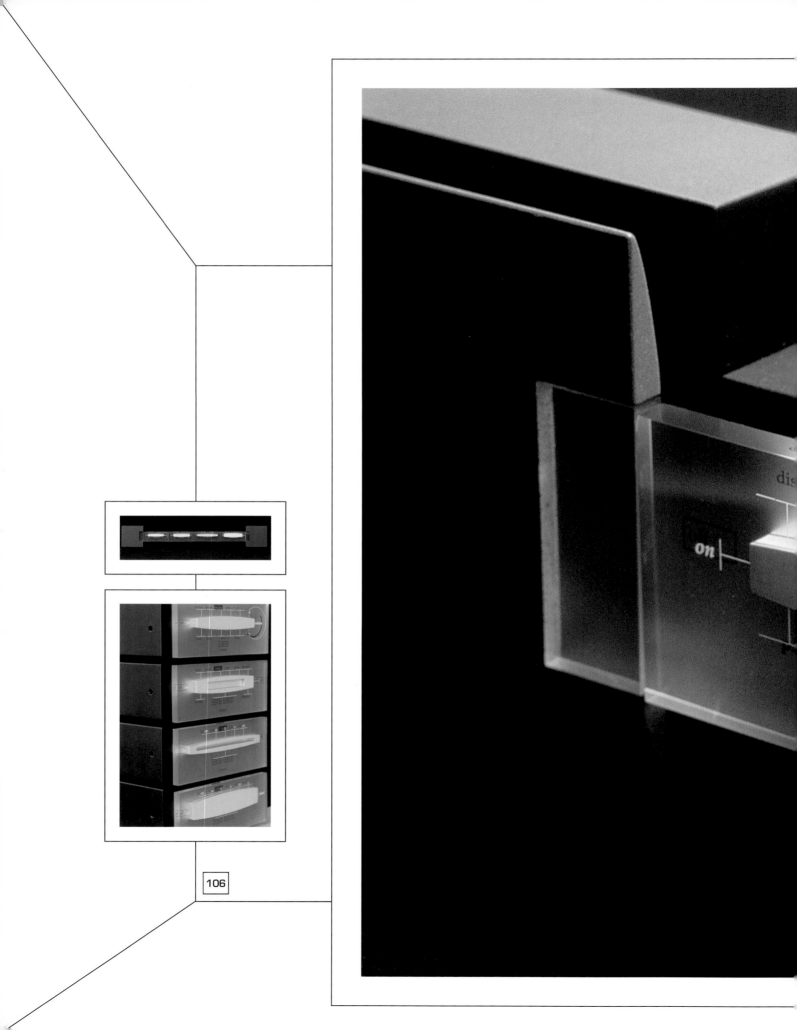

Having asked several designers to submit ideas for the latest Game Boy, manufacturer Nintendo selected Curiosity – a choice based partly on the outfit's playful approach to the perfume Le Feu d'Issey. Nicolas's task was to streamline the games computer into an accessible, contemporary toy. Although the basic shape was largely predetermined, Nicolas set about accentuating Game Boy's various functions. The previous model was characterised by its controls: one black cross and two round black buttons. The revised model has two extra buttons, which are manoeuvred by the left and right index fingers. Setting his sights on a unit that would be easier to hold, Nicolas proposed slightly more rounded lines and a larger and rounder frame for the LCD colour monitor. In his own words: 'My main contribution to the existing design was a hint of softness.'

    Initially, the people at Nintendo didn't like the idea of a white body, but Nicolas produced a convincing mock-up that helped to change their minds. He wanted an extremely simple design that wouldn't draw attention away from the software. The games themselves are colourful enough. The few bright accents that *are* featured on the case illustrate Game Boy's additional functions. Customers can select a white body with grey, green or blue accents. Reiko Miyamoto sees a lion's face in the design, a cat whose 'whiskers' reveal the product's speaker. A clever demonstration of her imagination, even though the average Nintendo player spots a lion only if it's part of the game and never stops to contemplate the frame that embraces the monitor.

nintendo game boy

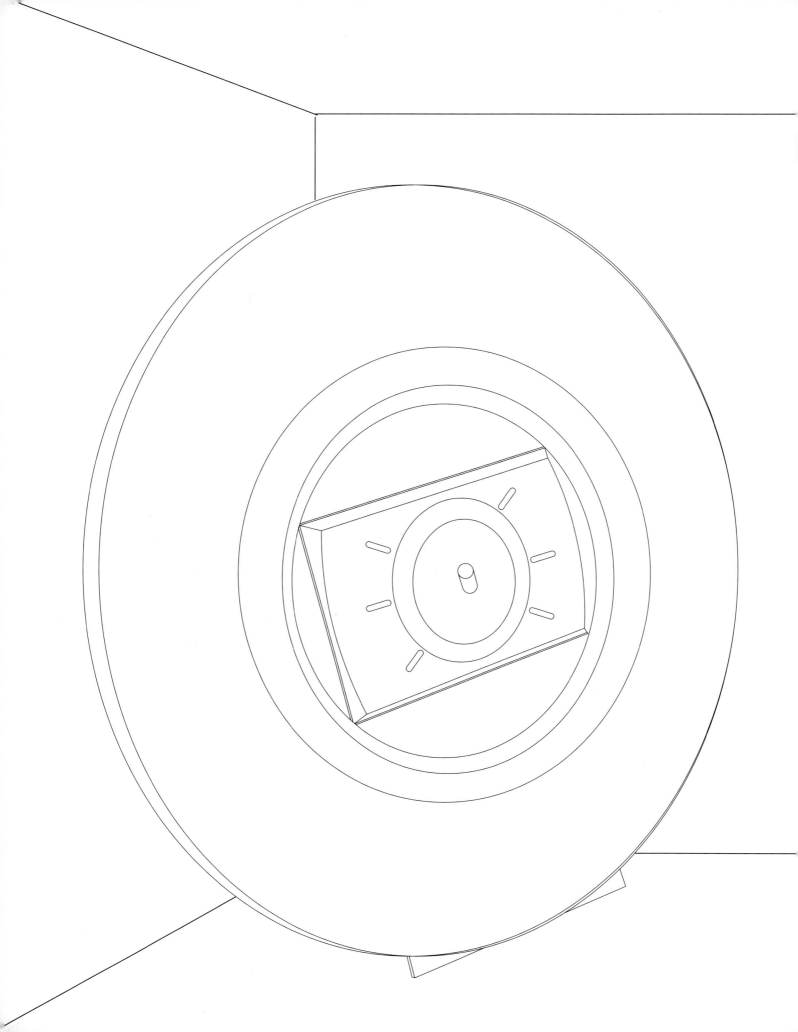

lg audio

Korean youth use portable cassette and CD players not only when they're on the go. At home they replace the headset with small speakers, thus transforming the street toy into a full-fledged stereo installation. When Korean firm Lucky Goldstar asked Naoki Sakai to develop a portable player with speakers for at-home use, the designer went to Nicolas for help. The latter decided to integrate charger and speakers into a single object. The result resembles a little picture frame with a wide rim, and, like a picture frame, it can stand on a flat surface or hang on the wall. The user clicks the set into the frame to charge the battery. With this component clicked in place, the combination becomes a stereo set, thanks to speakers concealed within the orange frame. The number of controls on the player has been reduced to one big button, which features a slide-and-turn mechanism that regulates all functions.

When Nicolas presented the concept in Korea, he used a bottle of Veuve Cliquot Champagne as a colour sample – realising, of course, that the client would be drawn not only to the bright-orange label. At the end of the meeting, they popped the cork and toasted the sparkling design.

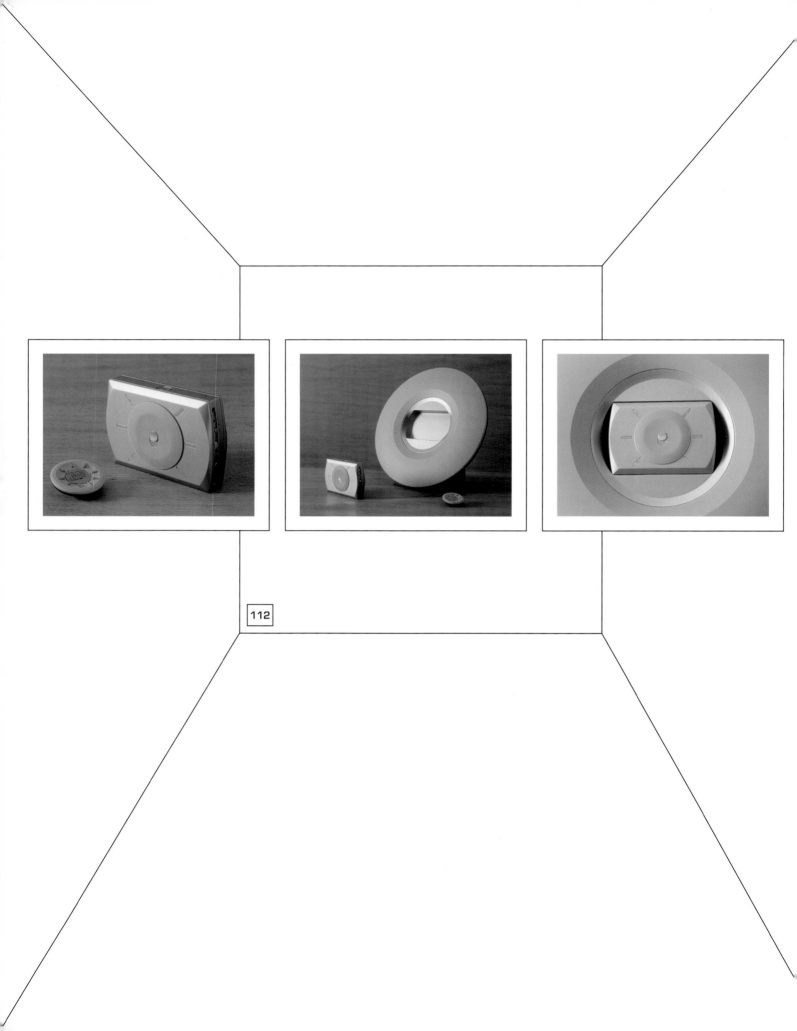

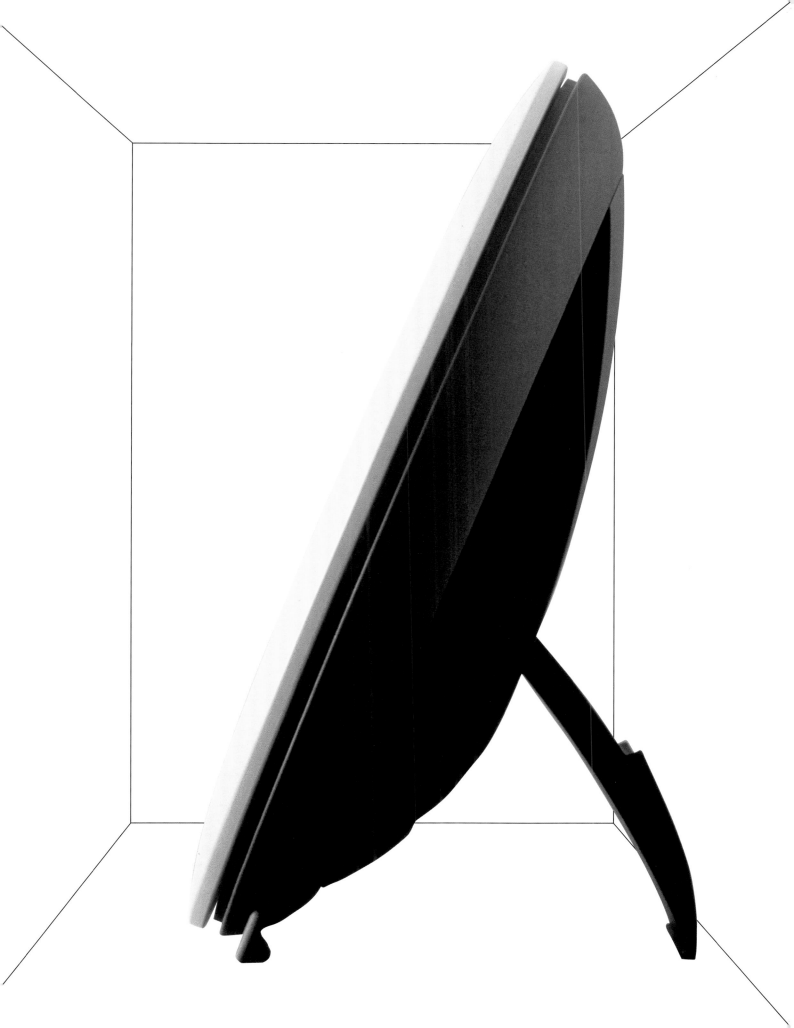

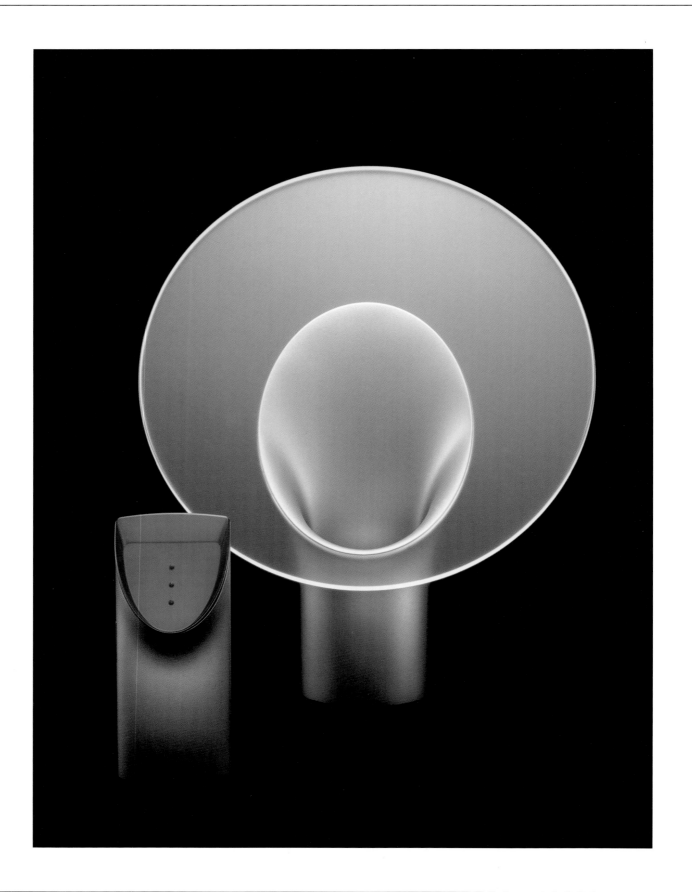

lg mobile phone

Smaller, lighter, with or without LCD or camera: the state of technology is a major determinant in the design of mobile phones. Thanks to the rapid development of colour LCDs, the small flip-style phone with a good-sized colour screen has become virtually the norm in Japan. A surprising development for a product that, prior to the i-mode era, looked more or less like a woman's compact.

The designers at Curiosity feel that mobile-phone manufacturers should review the situation and, while they're at it, pay more attention to design. In discussing the subject with Korean firm Lucky Goldstar, Nicolas ignored the cacophony of functions and based his prototype on the idea of a mobile phone as an ornament. Unintentionally, he designed a flip-style model that conceals its functions much as a compact does. The big difference lies in the frame of the device. The charger looks like a bizarre flower, which turns blue when the user inserts the phone.

A charger that doubles as a futuristically designed lamp? Manufacturers aren't ready for this one yet.

in pursuit of beauty

The thoughts of 'conceptor' Naoki Sakai, Gwenaël Nicolas's Japanese mentor and collaborator on more than forty projects, reveal the two faces of Curiosity's products. One speaks to logic and the other to emotion – the same distinction that separates technology from design.

'About ten years ago I got an interesting letter from Gwenaël Nicolas. Although I can't recall his exact words, I do remember comparing it to a love letter. The envelope held a tiny box with a seed in it. On the accompanying note, Nicolas had written: "Let's grow this seed together." The message conveyed a desire to work with me, and it illustrated his sense of humour. But my response to this off-the-wall approach was less than enthusiastic. To be honest, it made me feel uncomfortable. I had my secretary check him out before deciding what to do. She suggested I meet him, and I took her advice. Years later, I discovered that the letter he sent me was one of many. The story is a good introduction to Gwenaël. He never gives up. He's quite persistent, almost aggressive on occasion, but, at the same time, he has a gentle, charming personality. He just knows what he wants.

'At our first meeting, Gwenaël's portfolio consisted of academic projects, nothing more. I liked what I saw, however, and promised to keep in touch. About six months later I contacted him for a *butsudan* exhibition organised by the philosopher Seigo Matsuoka. Although the other participants were well-known architects, I thought that Nicolas – as a foreigner with no preconceived ideas about Japanese house altars – might have something new and interesting to contribute. The result was amazing. I was deeply impressed by his work. Since that time, Gwenaël has become almost a member of my family. I know what it's like to be alone in a foreign country. In the sixties, I led the life of a hippie in Los Angeles. The memory is still fresh.

'Interestingly, he met his future wife, Reiko Miyamoto, right here in my office at a little party for a product launch, a retro-style SW-1 Suzuki motorbike. Gwenaël and I have done more than forty projects together, including such disparate things as concept interiors for train carriages, digital cameras and telephone sets.

'Over the years, I've met a great many designers. In the nineties, after Japan's economic bubble burst, designers were hanging on by the skin of their teeth. It was a bitter struggle to survive. Gwenaël actually arrived in Japan during this harsh period. I must have met more than sixty foreign designers since that time, and as far as I know, he's the only success story in the lot – the only one who has managed to make a go of it in Tokyo.

'My work as a "conceptor" resembles that of a casting director. My clients are big companies in need of creative concepts for their products, but they rarely trust young unknown designers. Although not a designer

'Nicolas is a veritable goldmine of questions.
Why must form follow function? Why can't we limit the number
of functions? Or conceal them?'

myself, I have ideas about developing new products. As a reliable go-between, I'm familiar with the vocabulary of corporate Japan while also understanding the language spoken by designers. When asked to work on a concept, I have a pool of designers from which to select my cast.

'Nicolas springs to mind when the focus of a project is beauty, when the concept revolves around an object or idea that requires a strong visual impact. His products have two faces. One speaks to logic and the other to emotion. It's the same distinction that separates technology from design. Ultimately, however, he prefers the face of beauty. Sometimes he even claims – in no uncertain terms – to hate technology. With today's saturated market and no real competition in terms of price, beauty *is* the determining factor. And the popular desire for beauty may explain why Nicolas is so successful as an interior designer and in his work for Issey Miyake. In the world of fashion, design takes precedence over function. The same applies to many retail environments.

'Nicolas's strength may lie in the outward appearance of a product, but he doesn't take anything for granted. He's a veritable goldmine of questions. Why must form follow function in this particular case? Why can't we limit the number of functions? Or conceal them? "Curiosity" refers to more than the name that he and Reiko call their company. Having accepted his expertise in creating interiors, I still like to challenge him in the area of product design. And he invariably comes up with a surprise or two. Take the packaging design for Miyake's perfume, Le Feu d'Issey. Lift the bottle and the atomiser pops up automatically. It's a wonderful example of design in action – a product that communicates with the user.

'Nicolas has a terrific imagination and a wonderful insight into the future. About eight years ago, before 'internet' was a household word, Nissan asked us to design a concept car aimed at the year 2002. Instead of giving the manufacturer a flashy model that shouted 'designer-made', Gwenaël came up with a 2-metre-long pinball circuit that illustrated the integration of a local navigation system and a global positioning system and the influence of such integration on the functions found in automobiles. Not only was his highly entertaining presentation based on a great visual image; it also showed the workings of a very clever mind. We haven't yet been asked to design an entire car, bumper to bumper, but I'm anticipating such a project with relish. Automotive design is like architecture, but the manufacturing process makes it an even greater challenge. Exterior and interior design are equally important. Unlike the creation of mobile phones or PCs, for which a designer is hired to craft no more than a shell – in such cases, form *does* follow function – car design is relatively flexible. Standards are there to be changed. And I know precisely the actor I want to cast when the project calls for innovative standards.'

Naoki Sakai is a Japanese marketeer and 'conceptor', a term he coined for one who develops ideas for new products and services. Having founded Water Studio in 1973, he has collaborated for decades with creative minds that run the gamut of design: from architects and industrial designers to engineers and authors of haute couture. Cars like the Nissan Be-1, the Pao and the Rasheen are Sakai's brainchildren. He also developed the Emotional Program (EP), a marketing method for categorising consumers into nine groups according to lifestyle and an awareness of fashion brands.

In the urban landscape that is Tokyo, it's not unusual to come across huge spherical gas tanks in residential neighbourhoods. Even though these empty tanks are no longer considered a source of danger, they still face the threat of being dismantled. Gwenaël Nicolas thought it would be a pity not to give such perfectly formed structures a second chance. He went to the owner, Tokyo Gas, with the idea of creating a small alternative theatre-and-restaurant complex in the middle of the bustling city. After reluctantly providing Nicolas with technical specifications and drawings, the company also agreed to take him on a tour of the gas tanks.

Completely satisfied with the façades of the globular volumes, Nicolas concentrated exclusively on the interiors. His plans show that in the daytime, a passing glance at the exterior reveals little. Only after dark, when the great orbs are illuminated from below, do observers wonder what the mysterious complex holds in store.

Nicolas proposed simply sawing an entrance into one sphere, as if it were a do-it-yourself kit. To emphasise the circular form inside, he designed an inner skin that follows the rounded outline while not being directly attached to the wall of the tank. Because he was dealing with a temporary attraction that was not expected to last for decades, he opted for a less-than-flawless interior. The use of wood gives the otherwise metallic environment an added degree of intimacy, and the lack of an extra foundation under the wooden floors reinforces the impermanent, underground atmosphere that Nicolas was aiming for.

When the designer presented his plans to the gas company, Reiko Miyamoto agreed that transforming such a recognisable structure into a cultural centre would be good advertisement for the organisation. Unfortunately, Tokyo Gas did not share this conviction, and the complex remains unrealised.

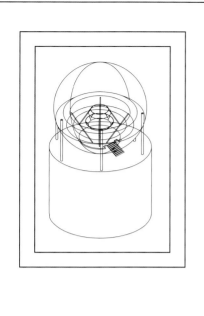

gas tank project

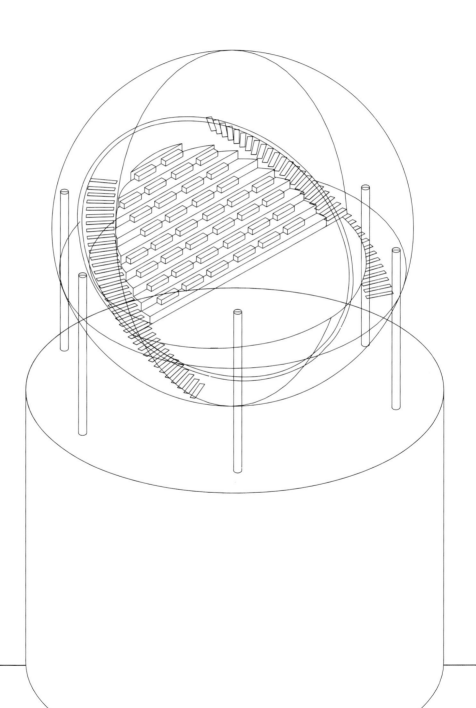

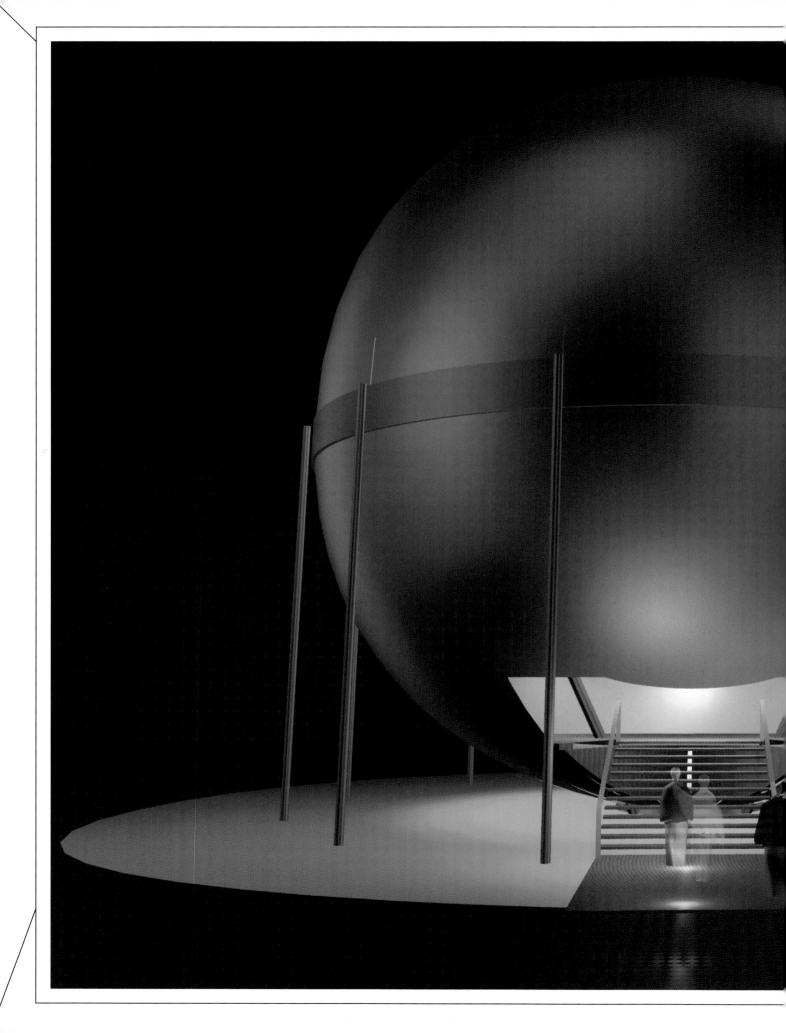

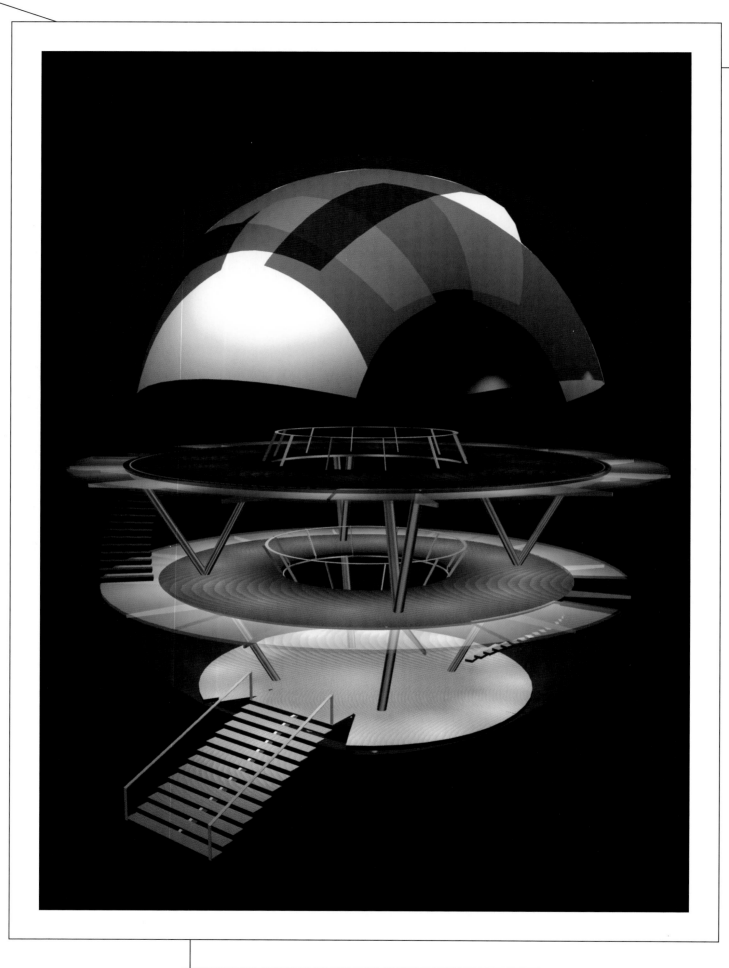

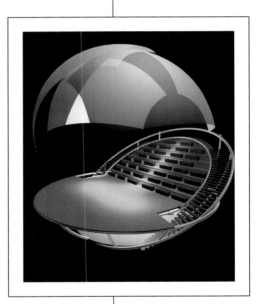

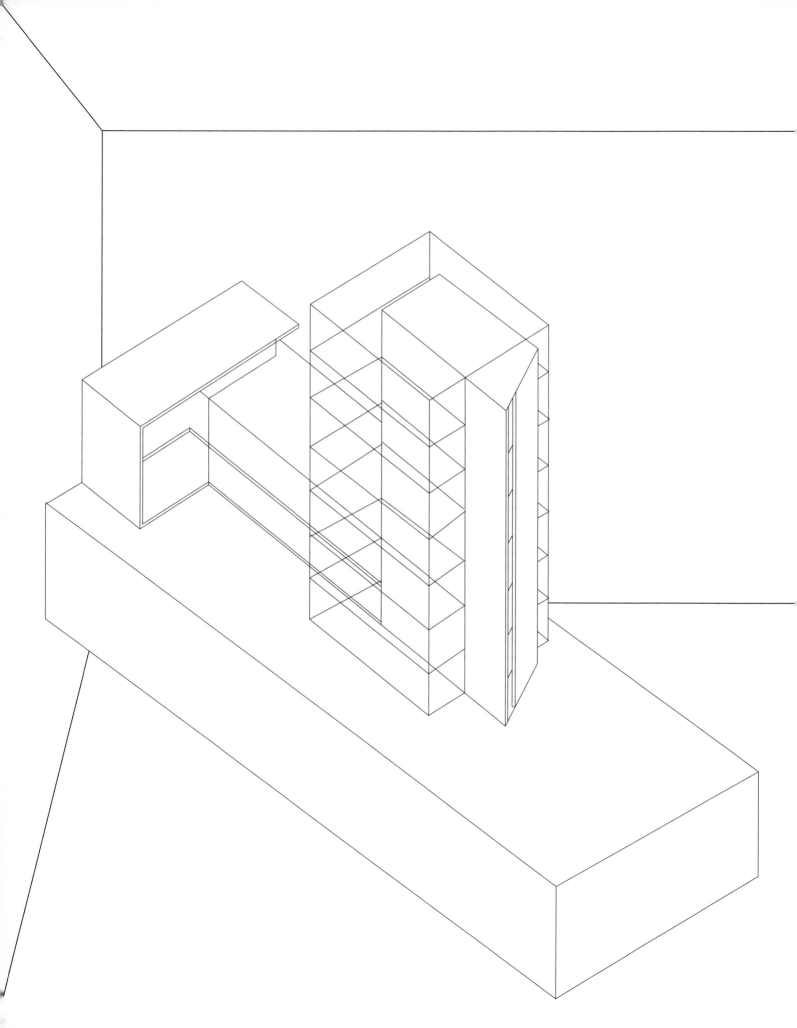

spa tokyo

On their own initiative, Gwenaël Nicolas and Reiko Miyamoto have been working on a design for a luxury bathhouse-cum-restaurant in the heart of Tokyo. The concept is based on the age-old Japanese tradition of the onsen, or thermal bath, a popular treat often combined with an exquisite dining experience and lodgings in a serene and scenic setting. In most cases, however, such spots are hours away from Tokyo, while virtually all spas in the Japanese metropolis are either examples of faded glory or additions to sports facilities. Time for a change, says the team at Curiosity.

The main building of the proposed complex consists of wood and glass. The front is completely panelled in wood, with the exception of an opening that runs the full height of the volume. This narrow cleft allows light to filter into the building while shielding the interior from the direct view of those passing by. It also helps to create an intriguing façade. Visitors pass the wooden panels, enter a space more than 10 metres high and leave the urban atmosphere behind. A sparsely furnished lobby, very natural in appearance, looks out on a narrow inner courtyard. A low corridor leads to a glass-clad restaurant at the rear of the complex, where one also finds lifts that lend access to the bathing facilities. The first floor accommodates thermal baths, saunas and jacuzzis, as well as rooms and cubicles for massage and beauty treatments. A second restaurant shares the top floor with a roof garden intended for relaxation and sunbathing.

Rooms and areas hosting various activities have high ceilings, while those in the hallways are low. Wherever the visitor stands, he catches a glimpse of an adjoining space; the clever layout directs him from one facility to another without imparting a sense of disorientation. A cosmetics label and a restaurant owner have already shown interest in the design.

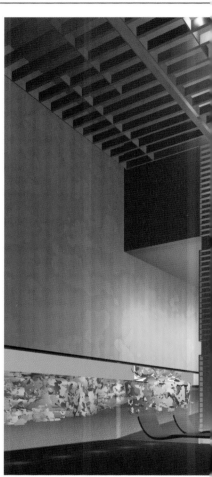

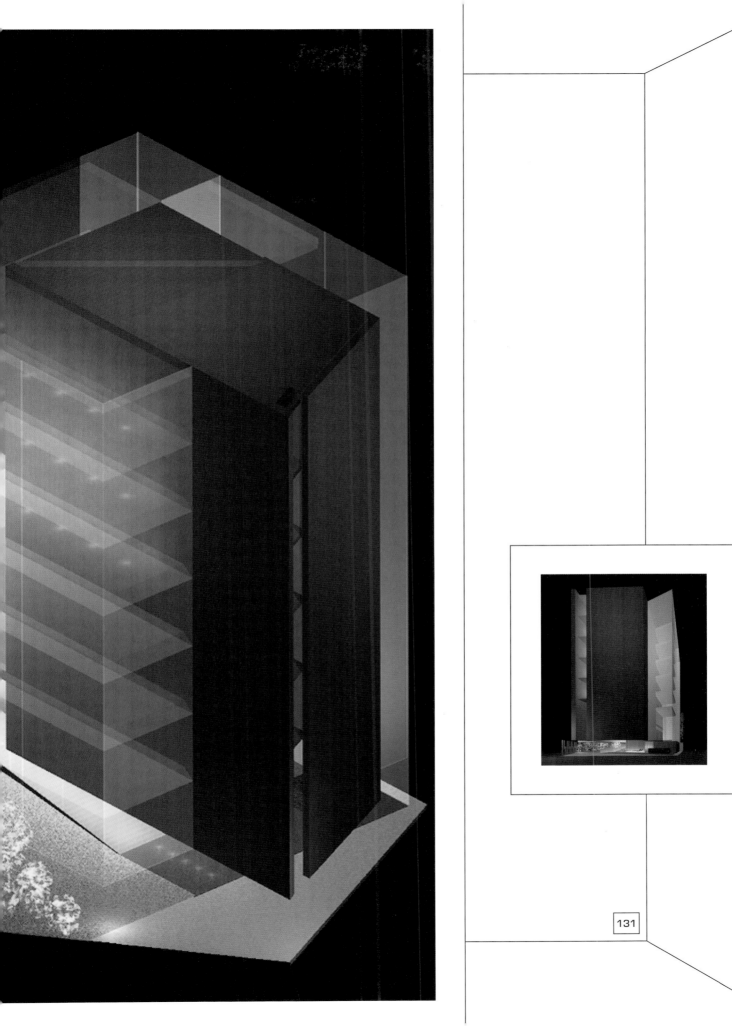

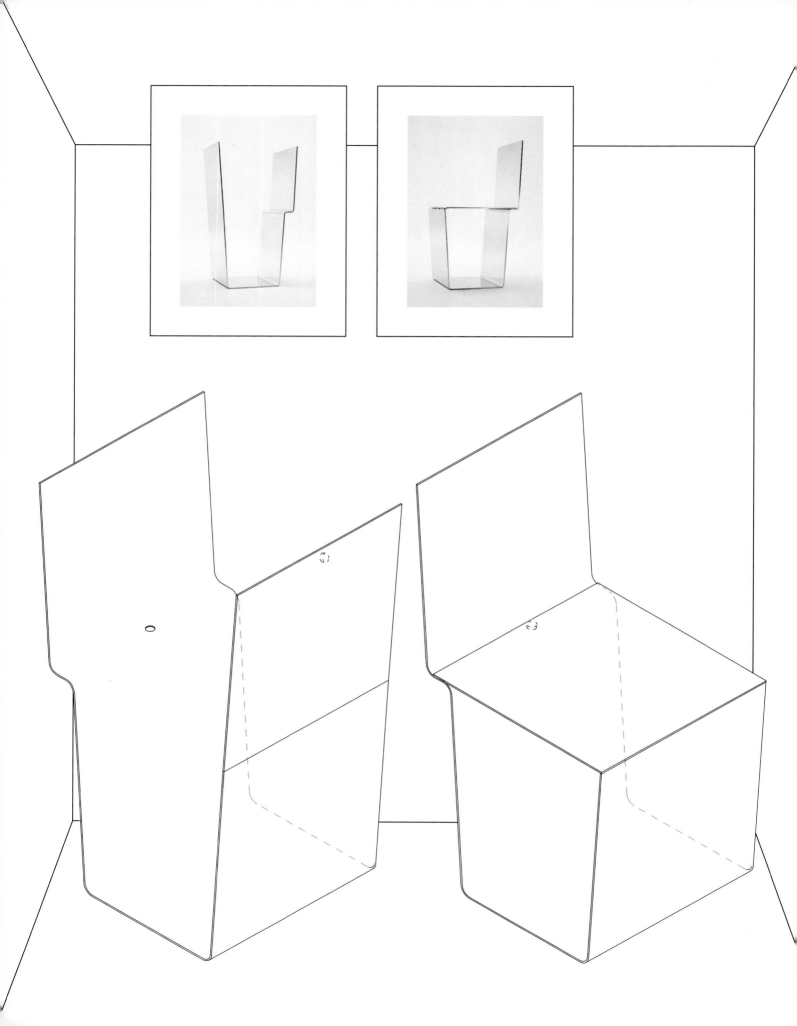

With his penchant for plain and simple forms, Nicolas designed a series of products which, when placed in an empty room, resemble an art installation or a contemporary sculpture. The idea originated while Nicolas was designing the Parallel chair for an exhibition. Without giving a thought to functionality, he began by developing a slender, elegant shape. He wanted to make an object that didn't immediately reveal its purpose. Two thin metal elements rise in parallel synchronicity. At the point where one meets the other halfway, it rests on a slightly protruding ridge. The result is a chair.

Nicolas embroidered on the following idea: rather than giving each new product a different form, take a pair of identical objects, build a relationship between the two and create a single product. With this concept in mind, he came up with a raft of twin objects; each duo forms a product. The two parts function only when connected to each other.

Throughout his studio are prototypal variations on this theme. Two buttonless white blocks are a stereo set with remote control. Twin blocks rocking on their sides become a pair of grey slippers when laid flat. Nicolas rotates a couple of wall-mounted blocks to make bookshelves and transforms thin, movable tubes into a source of light. Another interesting example is represented by the vertical treads of a stairway, all of which rotate 90 degrees when the first tread is moved into a horizontal position, creating a usable object.

Nicolas plans to organise an exhibition featuring the 'universe of parallels'. The idea is to divide the displays into two areas: one for the objects as abstract forms and one in which the same objects are coupled and presented as functional designs.

Almost a study of no-design, the exhibition will also be a reflection on the inflexibility with which many people look at products and their design.

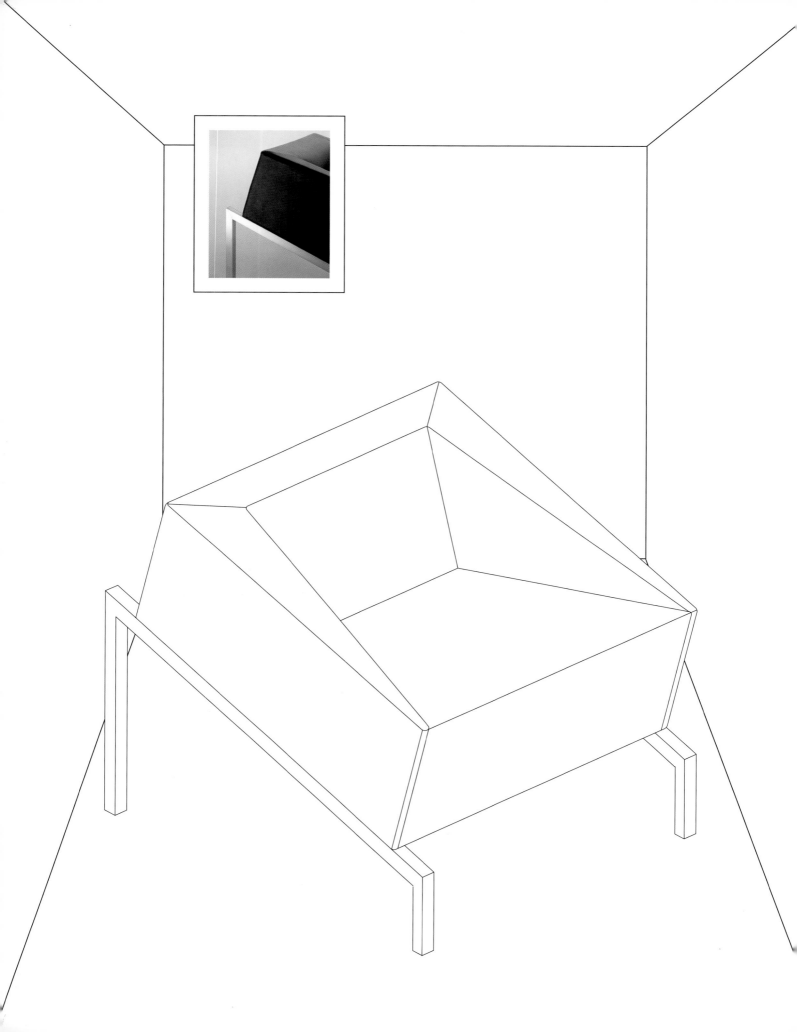

spider

A quintessentially classic design with a visual twist: the objective behind Gwenaël Nicolas's first attempt to design a sofa. According to Nicolas, people seated on a sofa often look a bit lost. They disappear, as it were, into a box. All that's clearly visible is a bunch of projecting body parts: two feet, two arms, a head. Nicolas set out to lift them from the box. The basic principle of a sofa – a piece of furniture with backrest, sides and seat – is at the heart of his design, but here all elements flow imperceptibly into one another. Although the angles formed by seat and backrest do not differ from those of ordinary sofas, in an optical sense they are not the same. This subtle twist eliminates the point of reference and thus appears to place the user quite comfortably on a raised platform. Doing exactly what he intended, Nicolas directs our attention to the seated rather than to the seat.

The Spider sofa looks like an oblique rectangle on legs. Strong but elegant. A monolithic structure. Not intended for domestic use, Spider belongs in the lobby of a major corporation or in a store. The image is too hard for a living room, says Nicolas. He had the design in his mind for some time before getting the opportunity to realise it for a shop interior. The exclusive prototype made its debut at the Takeo Kikuchi boutique. Variations on the design – a chair and a smaller sofa – have been manufactured on a small scale for Tag Heuer shops.

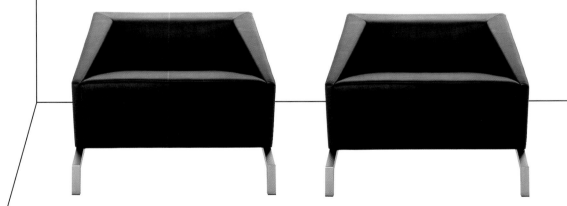

Issey Miyake wanted a marketplace atmosphere for his Pleats Please shop in Aoyama. Located on one of the few shopping squares in this fashionable Tokyo neighbourhood, the shop boasts an interior immersed in natural light. Apart from a striking curtain that covers one wall of the shop, Miyake's fashions are the only source of colour. Today the drape is pink, but its hue changes from season to season.

The fascinating part of this functional space lies in the details. A good example is the silver-grey floor at ground level, which is repeated one floor higher in a silvery ceiling that caps a virtually identical space. Nicolas created transparent tables and stools in varying heights for the display of accessories. Nothing distracts the customer's attention from the vivid fashions, with the exception of a ground-floor 'bridge' designed to give customers a shaky walk to their destination. Gasps of astonishment are followed by nervous giggles as visitors realise it's all part of the shopping experience.

Deciding whether to cross the bridge or descend a flight of stairs is the instant dilemma that faces a visitor entering the shop. Nicolas wanted the result to be a dynamic space that makes people want to browse around and touch the merchandise. He aimed for a layout that would lead them through the shop automatically, like an invisible map, while offering one multiple choice after another, along with various views of the products from different angles. From the look of things on a typical weekday – a flock of customers inspect, reflect and select – he seems to have achieved his goal.

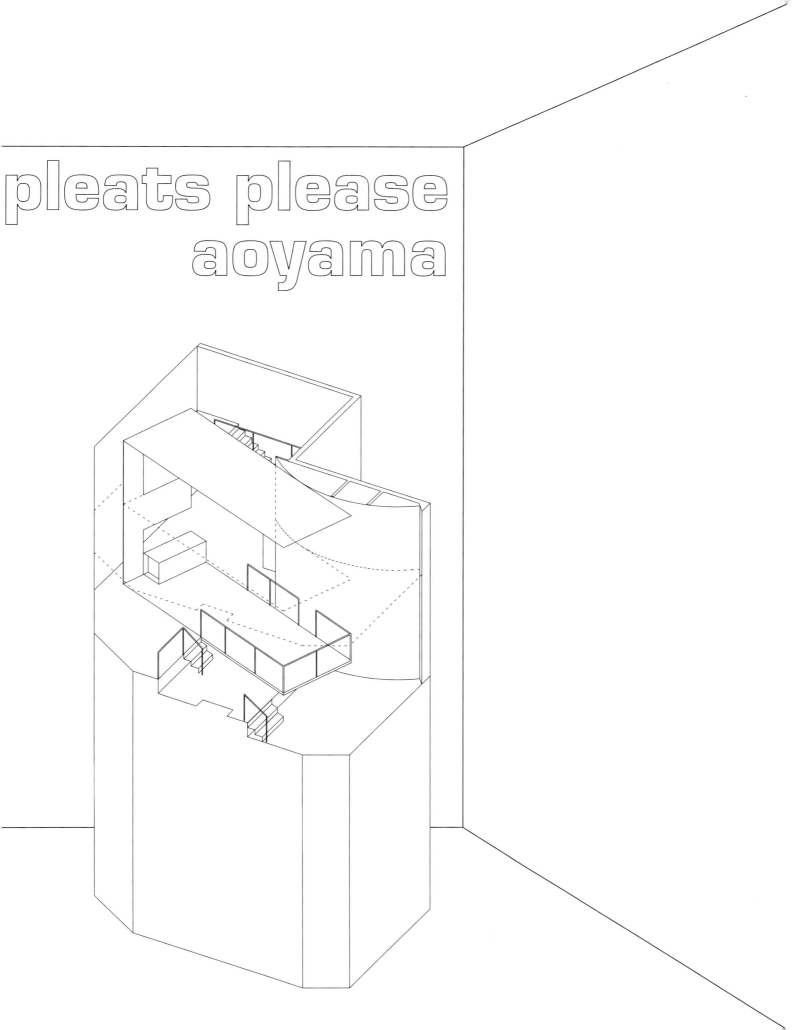

pleats please
aoyama

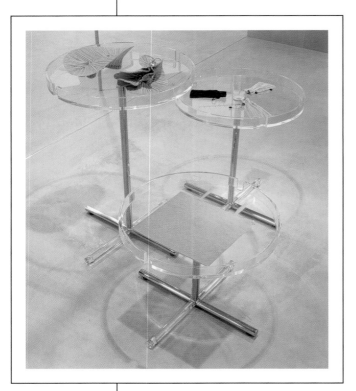

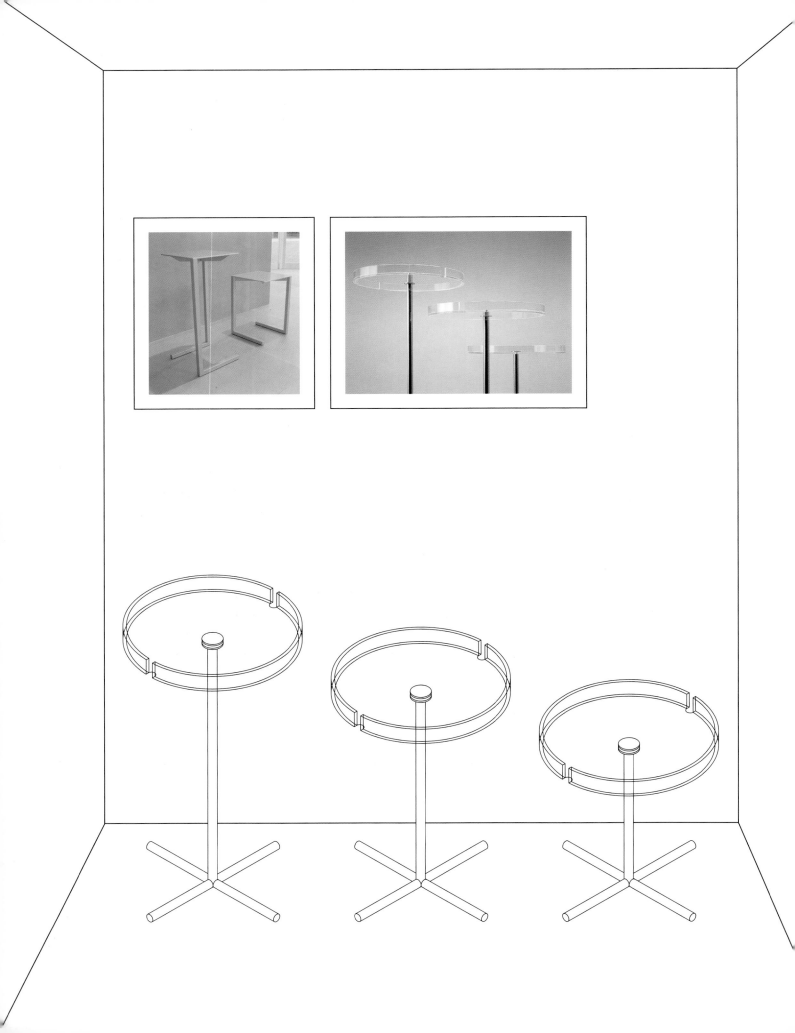

pink panther and flower

While working on Issey Miyake's Pleats Please shop in Aoyama, the fashion heart of Tokyo, Gwenaël Nicolas opted to design the furniture himself. Posing as high stools, three Pink Panthers stand at the counter. Indeed, the two-legged stool with its simple square seat looks more like an ingeniously balanced sculpture than like a place to sit.

Reiko Miyamoto took one look at the design, identified it as a walking chair and called it Pink Panther, a blatant reference to the humorous gait of the rosy cartoon kitty. Others had different ideas, as illustrated by the time that Curiosity took Pink Panther along to a presentation of the Boomerang sofa. Having used the stainless-steel stool as a colour sample for the legs of the sofa, Nicolas and Miyamoto left it at the Cassina office for the time being. Thinking that Pink Panther was the prototype for a new product, Cassina's sales staff christened it a 'side table'. Cassina is currently selling this chic little item, not without success, as a telephone table.

Nicolas also designed a set of three 'flower tables' for the Aoyama Pleats Please boutique. Well known for his colourful collections, Miyake had a bazaar in mind for this particular shop, a concept that Nicolas translated into no-nonsense display components of various sizes. Round acrylic tables of differing heights, which are used to show off a range of accessories, can be grouped in any number of ways. Thanks to notches in the transparent tabletops, the objects can be connected to one another like the petals of a flower. The notches are hardly noticeable when tables are used independently. Its raised edge makes the flower table an ultramodern display basket. Brightly coloured products placed on these one-legged tables form an irresistible temptation.

project credits

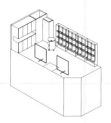

p 14

'me' Issey Miyake

Location

Matsuya Ginza 3F,
3-6-1 Ginza,
Chuo-ku, Tokyo
Client
Issey Miyake
General contractor
Ishimaru
Lighting design
Gwenaël Nicolas
Floor area
19m²
Start design
November 2000
Opening
February 2001
Materials
Floor: concrete
Wall: painted
plasterboard, glass
Ceiling: paint
Window: glass
Lighting fixtures:
Ushio Spax
Custom furnishings:
vending dispenser
(transparent acrylic),
counter (white
acrylic), clothes

hanger (transparent
acrylic)
Photography
Yasuaki Yoshinaga

p 14

'me' Issey Miyake
packaging
Client
Issey Miyake
Manufacturer
Issey Miyake
Start design
November 2000
Launch date
February 2001
Dimensions (w,h)
400 x 70mm
Material
PET

p 22

Pleats Please
St. Germain
Location
201 St Germain
Boulevard, Paris
Client
Issey Miyake
Lighting design
Gwenaël Nicolas
Floor area
50m²
Start design
1996
Opening
1996
Materials
Floor: limestone
Wall: paint
Ceiling: paint
Window: glass
Custom furnishings:
movable partition
(wood), showcase
(stainless steel), table
(stainless steel)
Photography
Yasuaki Yoshinaga

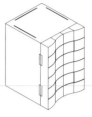

Boomerang

Client
Cassina Inter Décor
Producer
Waterstudio
Manufacturer
Cassina Inter Décor
Start design
2000
Launch date
October 2001
Dimensions (w,d,h)
sofa 1610 x 800 x
810mm; bench
1610 x 600 x 510mm
Materials
steel, PE foam,
upholstery used in
certain Honda cars
(brand Space Fabric)
Retail price
sofa ¥200,000;
bench ¥135,000

Tag Heuer Tokyo

Location
5-8-1 Jingumae,
Shibuya-ku, Tokyo
Client
Tag Heuer
General contractor
Ishimaru
Lighting design
Gwenaël Nicolas
Floor area
164m²
Start design
September 2000
Opening
October 2001
Materials
Floor: walnut, Alcilite
Wall: walnut, black
glass
Ceiling: plasterboard,
paint
Window: glass
Lighting fixtures:
Ushio Spax
Custom furnishings:
Spider chair (leather,
stainless steel),
counter (walnut),
showcase (walnut,

non-scratch acrylic),
panelling (walnut,
stainless steel),
low table (walnut,
stainless steel),
upholstered bench
(leather)
Photography
Nacása &
Partners/Daichi Ano

Butsudan

Client
O.M. Networks
Intermediary
Waterstudio
Manufacturer
O.M. Networks
Start design
1992
Launch date
1993
Dimensions (w,d,h)
400 x 500 x 600mm
Materials
wood, *kimpaku*
(Japanese art form
based on delicate
overlays of gold,
silver and copper),
black lacquer
Retail price
¥800,000

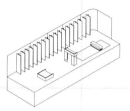 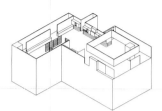

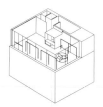 

 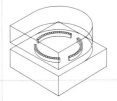

p 96	p 96	p 96	p 100
Le Feu d'Issey	Le Feu d'Issey travel pack	Le Feu d'Issey light	Le Feu d'Issey press launch
Client	**Client**	**Client**	**Location**
Beauté Prestige International	Beauté Prestige International	Beauté Prestige International	Tokyo Forum, Yurakucho, Tokyo
Manufacturer	**Manufacturer**	**Manufacturer**	**Client**
Beauté Prestige International	Beauté Prestige International	Beauté Prestige International	Beauté Prestige International
Start design	**Start design**	**Start design**	**General contractor**
1997	1998	2000	Ishimaru
Launch date	**Launch date**	**Launch date**	**Lighting design**
October 1998	October 1999	October 2000	Gwenaël Nicolas
Dimensions (w,d,h)	**Dimensions (w,d,h)**	**Dimensions (w,d,h)**	**Floor area**
700 x 700 x 900mm	600 x 600 x 600mm	700 x 700 x 900mm	300m²
Materials	**Materials**	**Materials**	**Start design**
glass, PCTA	glass, silicone rubber	glass, PCTA	1998
			Opening
			1998
			Materials
			Wall: white fabric (used as screen) Custom furnishings: round display counter with built-in lighting (wood, acrylic)
			Photography
			Masayoshi Inoue

Pioneer audio

Client

Pioneer
Intermediary

Producer

Waterstudio

Start design

1997

Launch date

prototype

Dimensions (w,d,h)

1100 x 200 x
200mm

Materials

glass, aluminium,
fabric

Nintendo Game Boy

Client

Nintendo

Manufacturer

Nintendo

Start design

May 2000

Launch date

March 2001

Dimensions (w,d,h)

145 x 25 x 800mm

Material

ABS

LG Audio

Client

LG Goldstar (Korea)

Producer

Waterstudio

Manufacturer

LG Goldstar (Korea)

Start design

1997

Launch date

1997

Dimensions (w,d,h)

350 x 100 x 350mm

Materials

plastics, fabric

LG Mobile phone

Client

LG Goldstar (Korea)

Start design

1998

Launch date

prototype

Dimensions (w,d,h)

250 x 100 x 300mm

Material

acrylic

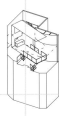

p 132
Parallel

Client
Original
Start design
March 2000
Dimensions (w,d,h)
300 x 300 x 650mm
Material
steel

p 134
Spider

Client
Original
Manufacturer
Ishimaru
Start design
December1999
Launch date
March 2000
Dimensions (w,d,h)
1500 x 900 x
650mm
Materials
steel, PE foam,
leather

p 138
Pleats Please Aoyama

Location
Minami Aoyama
Place, 3-13-21
Minami Aoyama,
Minato-ku, Tokyo
Client
Issey Miyake
General contractor
Ishimaru
Lighting design
Gwenaël Nicolas
Floor area
200m²
Start design
February 2000
Opening
April 2000
Materials
Floor: Alcilite,
concrete
Wall: paint
Curtain: neoprene
Ceiling: Alcilite, paint
Window: glass
Lighting fixtures:
Ushio Spax
Custom furnishings:
stool (steel), counter
(Alcilite), showcase

(transparent acrylic),
sofa (stretch-fabric
cover), accessories
table in three
heights (acrylic)
Photography
Shinicho Sato

Pink Panther

Client

Issey Miyake

Manufacturer

Ishimaru

Start design

March 2000

Launch date

April 2000

Dimensions (w,d,h)

300 x 300 x 600mm

Material

steel

p 146

Flower

Client

Issey Miyake

Manufacturer

Ishimaru

Start design

March 2000

Launch date

April 2000

Dimensions (w,d,h)

300 x 300 x 600mm

Material

steel

158

PIRATES
AND
PIONEERS

Philip Steele and Mike Stotter

KING*f*ISHER

CONTENTS

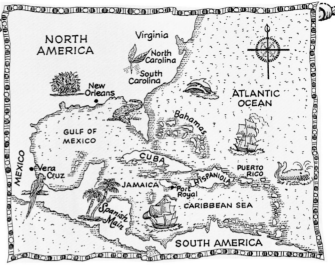

KINGFISHER
Kingfisher Publications Plc
New Penderel House, 283–288 High Holborn,
London WC1V 7HZ
www.kingfisherpub.com

Material in this edition previously published by Kingfisher
Publications Plc in the *Best-Ever* series

This edition published by Kingfisher Publications Plc 2001
10 9 8 7 6 5 4 3 2 1

1TR/0501/TWP/UNIV(MAR)/150SIN

Copyright © Kingfisher Publications Plc 1997

A CIP catalogue record for this book is available from the British
Library.

ISBN 0 7534 0617 9

Printed in Singapore

INTRODUCTION

 The story of pirates and pioneers begins in the late 15th-century, when Europeans first discovered the Americas and the West Indies. Rewards could be huge for those who braved life in foreign climes – perhaps land rich in oil or gold. Ordinary people were attracted to these wealthy lands and began to set up homes and trading stations. But the prospect of easy money also lured pirates. Money-making opportunities meant that there was much competition for the land and treasure, and law and order were not always maintained. Life was a dangerous gamble for both pirates and pioneers...

LAND AHOY! After many long and arduous months at sea, it was a relief to travellers when land was finally spotted on the horizon.

5

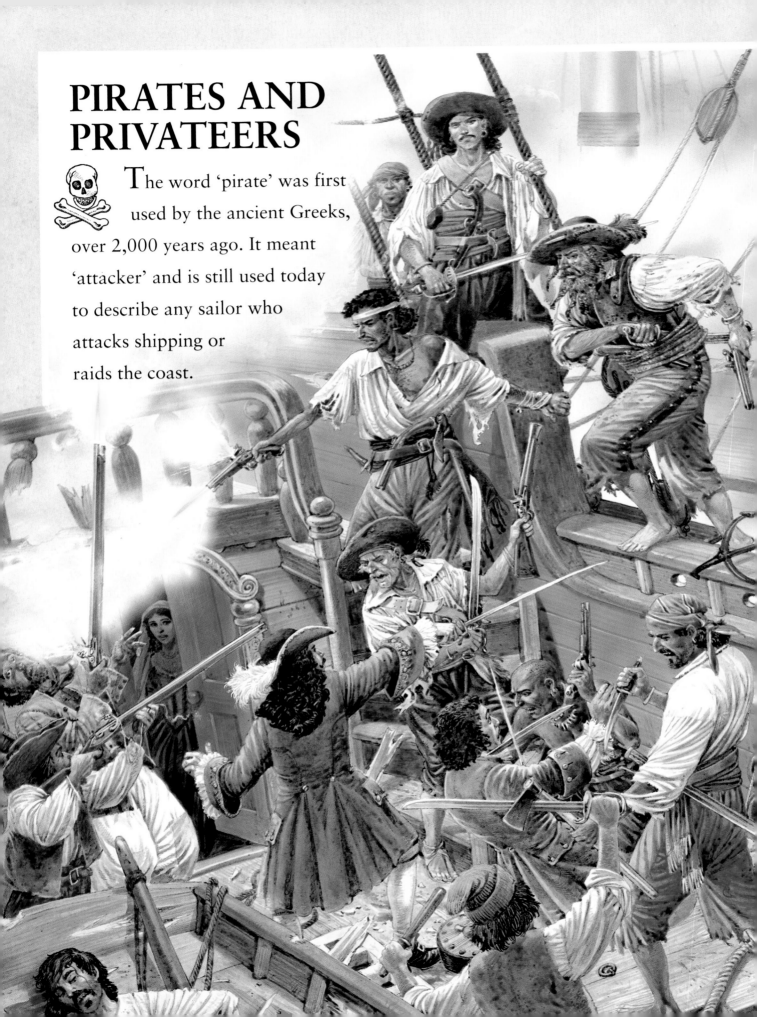

PIRATES AND PRIVATEERS

The word 'pirate' was first used by the ancient Greeks, over 2,000 years ago. It meant 'attacker' and is still used today to describe any sailor who attacks shipping or raids the coast.

◀ Buccaneers swarm over a merchant ship. These pirates terrorized shipping in the Caribbean Sea between about 1630 and 1697. Many were brutal and greedy murderers, but others were desperate men who had little choice but to live as pirates. It was their only way of avoiding a miserable life as sailors or poor plantation workers. The Caribbean pirates of 300 years ago included Africans who had escaped from slavery, as well as outlaws from Europe and the Americas.

▲ This old chart shows Francis Drake's attack on Cartagena, Colombia, in 1586. Four hundred years ago, Cartagena was a port for the Spanish treasure fleet.

In 1581 Queen Elizabeth I had made Francis Drake a knight. To the English, Drake was a national hero. To the Spanish, he was nothing but a common pirate.

Many other words have been used to describe pirates. Corsairs, buccaneers, rovers, filibusters and freebooters... all were pirates of one kind or another. Sometimes governments licensed private ship-owners to attack the merchant vessels of another country with whom they were at war. These lawful pirates were called 'privateers' and they shared the profits with the government. Many respectable seafarers like Francis Drake turned pirate from time to time. And many governments secretly supported pirate expeditions – provided the pirates shared the booty with them!

Clues to the past

How do we find out the truth about piracy? Many tales about pirate captains and buried treasure are little more than tall stories. How can we prove when and where a ship was sunk? On land, archaeologists can dig up remains from the past and find out how old they are. Marine archaeology is harder. Shipwrecks may be buried or scattered. Divers may have to work in dangerous conditions in deep water.

▼ How do divers know which ship they have found? At this wreck, the ship's bell was engraved with the words THE WHYDAH GALLY 1716.

Marine archaeology
The English ship *Whydah* traded in slaves, sugar, indigo dye and ivory. In February 1717, the ship was captured by the pirate Sam Bellamy. It went down during a storm off Cape Cod, North America, in April 1717. The *Whydah* sank in shallow water, but for 266 years it lay hidden in deep sand.

Piratical documents

Some buccaneers of the 1600s and 1700s, such as Basil Ringrose and William Dampier, left behind logbooks, charts and stories of their travels. The most famous account was *Bucaniers of America* by the French buccaneer Alexandre Exquemelin, which was first published in Amsterdam in 1678.

◀ **The wreck of the *Whydah* was eventually discovered by an American diver called Barry Clifford in 1983. Instead of its normal cargo, it contained Sam Bellamy's pirate treasure of gold and silver coins, gold bars, parts of swords, muskets and pistols, cannons and grenades, and a leather pouch and shoe.**

Another way we can find out about the past is by reading old inscriptions, gravestones and books. But we cannot believe every word we read. Some writers exaggerated the facts, or claimed that their enemies were pirates when they weren't. There are other references to piracy in old law books and reports of trials and executions. In the 1600s and early 1700s, the lands of North America and the Caribbean were colonies, ruled by European nations. Colonial governors sent in reports about piracy, and these can still be read today.

Found on land

Archaeology on dry land tells us about the daily life of pirates ashore. Many had bases in ports or on remote islands around the world.

Rum bottles, tankards, candlesticks, spoons and brass buckles were discovered at Port Royal, the Jamaican pirate base destroyed by an earthquake in 1692.

Treasure fleets

The mainland of Central and South America was known as 'the Spanish Main'. This name was later used for the whole Caribbean. From the 1540s onwards, the Spanish organized two naval convoys each year to protect the ships carrying all the treasure back home. One left from Vera Cruz and the other from Nombre de Dios (or later from Portobello). The two convoys joined forces off Cuba for the voyage back to Spain. The combined fleet could number up to 100 vessels. The treasure was transported in ships called galleons, which could carry 200 crew and 60 cannon. Few pirate ships could match them, but pirates had the advantage when it came to speed and cunning.

▶ In June 1523 a French corsair called Jean Fleury (or Florin) was prowling the Atlantic shipping lanes off Cape St Vincent, near Faro in Portugal. He sighted three unescorted caravels, small three-masted vessels bound for Spain.

Fleury closed on the ships and managed to capture two of them, although the third escaped.

The Spanish caravels were loaded with vast amounts of treasure seized from the Aztecs, a Native American people who lived in what is now Mexico. The powerful Aztec empire had been defeated by a Spanish soldier, Hernando Cortés, in 1521. Fleury's attack on the Spanish treasure fleet was the first of many by French and English corsairs.

A NEW WORLD

On October 12, 1492 an Italian seafarer, Christopher Columbus, landed on Watling's Island in the Bahamas. Columbus was in the service of the King and Queen of Spain, and thought he had reached part of Asia. In fact he had landed in the Americas, a 'new world' unknown to Europeans. In the years that followed, Spain seized vast areas of land in the Americas.

Many Native Americans were enslaved, murdered or died of disease. Gold and silver were shipped back to Europe. Plantations were set up on the Caribbean islands, and these were worked by poor Europeans and African slaves. This combination of desperate men, remote islands and Spanish treasure could only lead to one thing – piracy.

▶ Francis Drake was an English privateer who often broke the rules to engage in piracy. From 1567 to 1596 he led one attack after another on the Spanish fleet, capturing a vast fortune in gold. In 1572, when England was supposed to be at peace with Spain, Drake attacked Nombre de Dios.

Brethren of the Coast

In the 1600s large numbers of wild adventurers and outlaws took refuge in the Caribbean. They came from the Netherlands, the British Isles, France, Portugal, West Africa and from the Caribbean islands themselves. Some were known as 'buccaneers', others as 'Brethren of the Coast'. At first they lived on Cuba, Jamaica and Hispaniola. From the 1630s, their chief base was the island of Tortuga.

Barbecued pig
The buccaneers took their name from the *boucan*, or smoke-house, in which they cooked meat. Raw meat was placed over a wood-chip fire and preserved by the clouds of smoke.

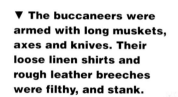

▼ The buccaneers were armed with long muskets, axes and knives. Their loose linen shirts and rough leather breeches were filthy, and stank.

▶ The buccaneers lived outside the law, brawling and shooting. They were often drunk on rum and brandy. The early buccaneers lived in rough, open-air camps and hunted wild pigs and cattle with dogs. They traded the meat and hides of the animals they hunted for gunpowder and supplies.

| Roche Brasiliano | François l'Ollonois | Bartolomeo el Portugués |

Three madmen

Some mad and violent buccaneers took pride in acts of cruelty. Roche Brasiliano, a Dutch captain, roasted his enemies alive. Jean-David Nau, a Breton better known as François l'Ollonois, hacked out the heart of a Spanish captive and tore it with his teeth. Bartolomeo the Portuguese was a notorious murderer.

The colonial governors soon had enough of the lawless buccaneers. They tried to stop their trade in cattle and pig meat, so the buccaneers decided to become pirates. By the 1660s they were launching fierce attacks on the Spanish treasure ships. This suited Spain's enemies very well. They began to hire buccaneer armies to plunder Spanish towns on the mainland. The great age of buccaneering lasted into the 1690s, and the pirates' fame spread around the world.

▲ The mainland of Central and South America stayed under Spanish rule during the 1650s, but in the Caribbean Spain's power was challenged by the British and French – and by pirates of all nations who used the islands to hide from the law.

▶ The buccaneers attacked Spanish galleons from dugout canoes, or *piraguas*. These were fast, and a difficult target for enemy cannon.

13

Port Royal, Jamaica

In 1655 Britain seized the Caribbean island of Jamaica from the Spanish. The newcomers did not have enough troops to hold the island against a Spanish or French attack, so they struck a deal with the buccaneers. The pirates could anchor at Port Royal and frighten off enemy shipping. The most famous buccaneer to base himself in Port Royal was a Welsh rogue called Henry Morgan. Morgan was given official backing to raid Spanish towns on the mainland.

◄ Port Royal in the 1660s became famous for its lawlessness. The smelly streets of the port were filled with drunken merchants, cruel slave traders, sailors with squawking parrots, gamblers and rogues, and swaggering buccaneers.

Morgan's raids
Between 1668 and 1671 Henry Morgan led his men on raids against Puerto Principe, Portobello, Maracaibo, and Panama.

Henry Morgan was now a privateer who could raise large armies from amongst the buccaneers. Because of this, the colonial authorities in Jamaica chose to ignore his illegal acts of piracy and cruelty. He was knighted by King Charles II and was even made Lieutenant Governor of Jamaica. A heavy drinker, Morgan died in 1688. After his death the colony no longer needed its unruly buccaneers. Indeed, Port Royal now became famous as the place where pirates were captured, tried and hanged.

God's punishment?

On June 7, 1692 the busy streets and wharves of Port Royal suddenly fell silent. And then the whole earth shook and rumbled. Taverns collapsed and warehouses packed with sugar and tobacco fell into the harbour. The sea flooded into the town. As news of the earthquake spread, people claimed that Port Royal was being punished for its sins.

Women pirates

Three pirates were among many brought to trial in Jamaica in November 1720. One, John Rackham, was found guilty and hanged. The other two were found guilty, but were let off – when the court found that they were both expecting babies. Their names were Mary Read and Anne Bonny. Read and Bonny had been brought up as boys, so they were used to dressing in men's clothes and found them better suited to life at sea. They fought violently with cutlasses, axes and pistols, and became the best known women pirates of all time.

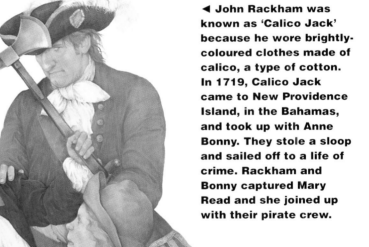

◄ John Rackham was known as 'Calico Jack' because he wore brightly-coloured clothes made of calico, a type of cotton. In 1719, Calico Jack came to New Providence Island, in the Bahamas, and took up with Anne Bonny. They stole a sloop and sailed off to a life of crime. Rackham and Bonny captured Mary Read and she joined up with their pirate crew.

North American waters

While the Spanish ruled the Caribbean and the Pacific coasts, British colonists settled along the eastern coast of North America. They had to pay high taxes to the government back home for many of the goods they imported. In the 1700s, some settlers got their own back by taking up smuggling and piracy. They preyed on shipping from Newfoundland down to the Carolinas, and often even farther away. Some colonial governors could be persuaded to take no notice, provided they were given a share of the profits.

Down in New Orleans

Jean Lafitte was a notorious pirate and smuggler who controlled every racket in New Orleans. When the United States went to war against Britain in 1812, Lafitte turned down an offer of money from the British. Instead he offered his services to American officers and became a privateer – and a hero.

▼ Appearing like some demon from hell, Blackbeard showed no mercy. His ship, the *Queen Anne's Revenge*, attacked ships off South Carolina and blockaded the prosperous port of Charleston.

Stede Bonnet

Stede Bonnet was a respectable, middle-aged gentleman who had a reputation as a dandy. He had retired from the army and owned a plantation in Barbados. Feeling depressed, or perhaps just bored with life, Bonnet turned pirate captain. For a time he sailed with Blackbeard's fleet, where he became a figure of fun. In 1718 Bonnet was captured and hanged in Charleston.

After Port Royal was cleaned up, Nassau on New Providence Island in the Bahamas attracted thousands of pirates. They lived riotously and joined the attack on Atlantic shipping. In 1775, war broke out between Britain and her American colonies. The Americans had only a small navy, so they relied on privateers to attack British merchant ships. By 1783 the Americans had trounced the British and formed an independent nation – the United States.

Blackbeard's terror

The most feared pirate in North America from 1716 onwards was Bristol-born Edward Teach, known as 'Blackbeard'. He was a brutal man who wore his hair and beard in long plaited 'dreadlocks'. He tied smouldering fuses under his hat to terrify his victims.

▶ In November 1718 Governor Alexander Spotswood of Virginia offered £100 for the capture of Blackbeard. It was Lieutenant Robert Maynard of HMS *Pearl* who killed the pirate, in a desperate hand-to-hand fight. He cut off Blackbeard's head and hung it from the bowsprit.

COASTS OF AFRICA

Most of Africa remained unknown to the outside world until the 1800s. Medieval maps were often left blank, or covered with pictures of lions. Rich empires existed inland, but few explorers survived the long journeys through deserts and jungles to reach them.

▼ The Welsh pirate captain Bartholomew Roberts checks his haul of treasure by the Senegal River in 1721. Roberts was one of the most successful pirates of all time, capturing or sinking over 400 ships.

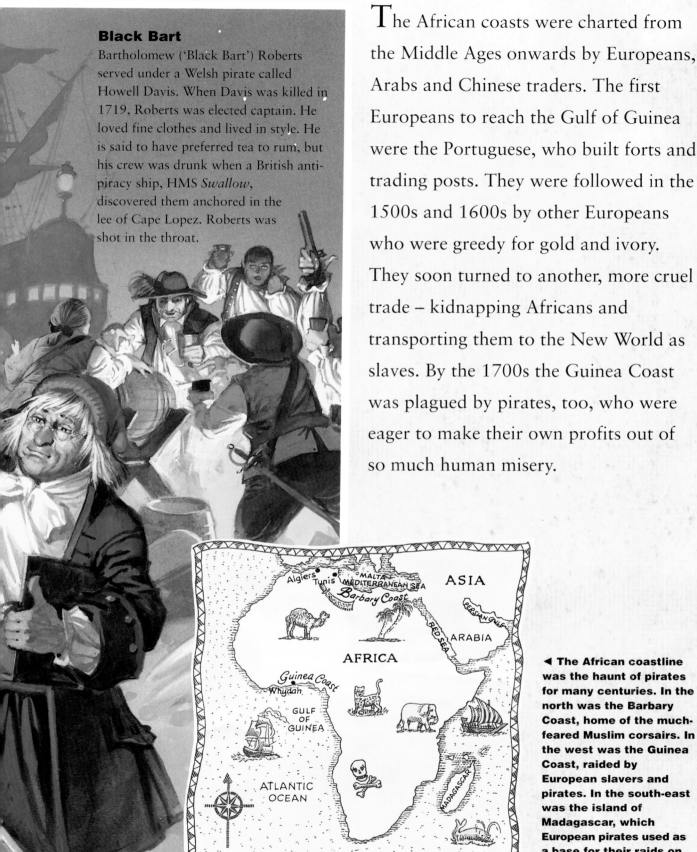

Black Bart

Bartholomew ('Black Bart') Roberts served under a Welsh pirate called Howell Davis. When Davis was killed in 1719, Roberts was elected captain. He loved fine clothes and lived in style. He is said to have preferred tea to rum, but his crew was drunk when a British anti-piracy ship, HMS *Swallow*, discovered them anchored in the lee of Cape Lopez. Roberts was shot in the throat.

The African coasts were charted from the Middle Ages onwards by Europeans, Arabs and Chinese traders. The first Europeans to reach the Gulf of Guinea were the Portuguese, who built forts and trading posts. They were followed in the 1500s and 1600s by other Europeans who were greedy for gold and ivory. They soon turned to another, more cruel trade – kidnapping Africans and transporting them to the New World as slaves. By the 1700s the Guinea Coast was plagued by pirates, too, who were eager to make their own profits out of so much human misery.

◄ The African coastline was the haunt of pirates for many centuries. In the north was the Barbary Coast, home of the much-feared Muslim corsairs. In the west was the Guinea Coast, raided by European slavers and pirates. In the south-east was the island of Madagascar, which European pirates used as a base for their raids on ships in the Indian Ocean.

Pirate kingdoms

Other African coasts were notorious centres of piracy. In the 1600s, Dutch, French and Portuguese pirates cruised the shores of southern Africa. Soon pirates were sailing all the way from North America to Africa and up the Red Sea – a route that became known as 'the Pirate Round'. From 1690 until 1720 the pirates' chief base was Madagascar. Rumours spread about the easy life to be had on the island, about the beautiful women and tropical sunshine. But the life led by Madagascar pirates was really a tough one.

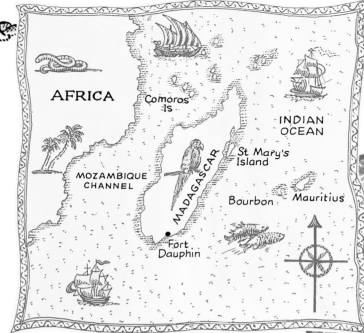

▲ This map shows Madagascar, chief port of call on the Pirate Round. The island became a place where pirates took on food and water or sold cargoes they had captured in the Indian Ocean.

Too kind by half

Pirate captains were not often known for their kindness. The Irish pirate Edward England operated on the Guinea Coast and in the Indian Ocean. But when he let a British merchant captain sail off unharmed, England's crew were disgusted and dumped him in Mauritius. He built a small boat and rowed all the way to Madagascar.

▼ Careening took place when a ship was beached for repairs. This was the moment when pirates were most at risk from attack. They camped on the shore and had no means of escape.

In tropical waters the hulls of wooden ships soon became covered with barnacles and weed and were riddled with holes made by marine worms. Pirates stopped at St Mary's Island, off Madagascar, to repair their ships.

Daniel Defoe (1661–1731) wrote of a new country called Libertalia, founded on Madagascar by a pirate called Captain Misson. It probably never existed, but other Madagascar pirates did declare themselves local rulers. There was 'King' Abraham Samuel in the 1690s and James Plantain, 'King of Ranter Bay', in the 1720s.

Tools of the trade

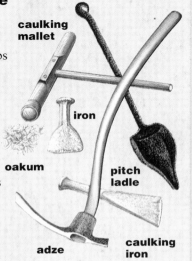

An adze was used to shape wood into new planks. The seams (gaps between the planks) then had to be caulked (filled). So they were forced open with an iron and packed with oakum (fibres pulled out of ropes). This was hammered in with a mallet and caulking iron and then daubed with pitch, or tar.

caulking mallet

iron

oakum

pitch ladle

adze

caulking iron

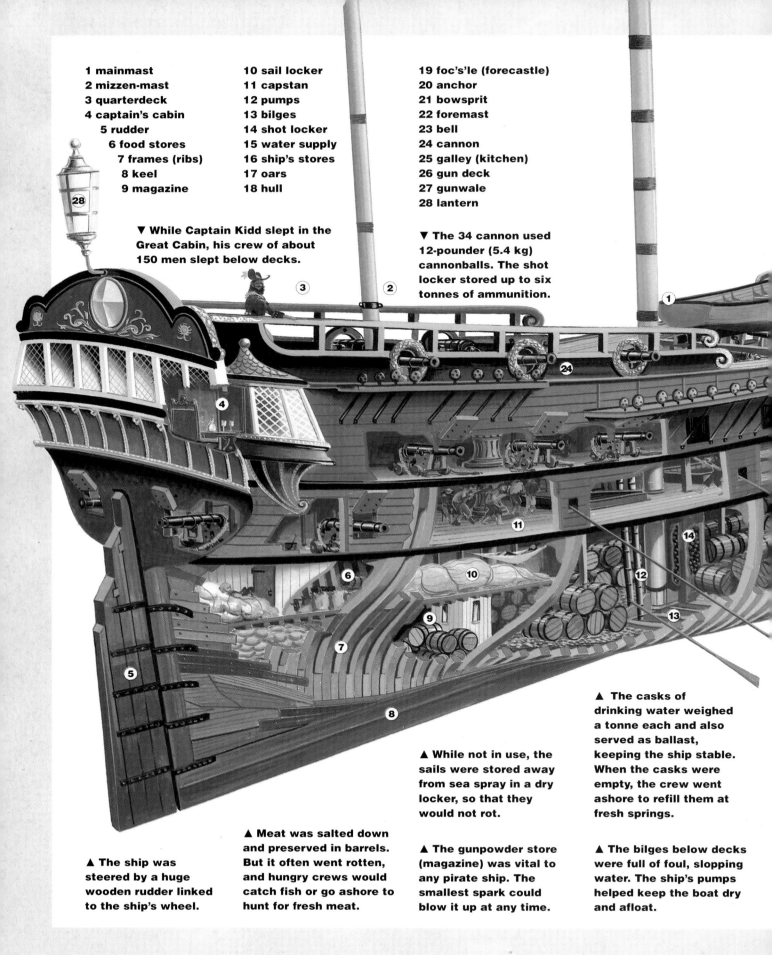

1 mainmast
2 mizzen-mast
3 quarterdeck
4 captain's cabin
5 rudder
6 food stores
7 frames (ribs)
8 keel
9 magazine
10 sail locker
11 capstan
12 pumps
13 bilges
14 shot locker
15 water supply
16 ship's stores
17 oars
18 hull
19 foc's'le (forecastle)
20 anchor
21 bowsprit
22 foremast
23 bell
24 cannon
25 galley (kitchen)
26 gun deck
27 gunwale
28 lantern

▼ While Captain Kidd slept in the Great Cabin, his crew of about 150 men slept below decks.

▼ The 34 cannon used 12-pounder (5.4 kg) cannonballs. The shot locker stored up to six tonnes of ammunition.

▲ The ship was steered by a huge wooden rudder linked to the ship's wheel.

▲ Meat was salted down and preserved in barrels. But it often went rotten, and hungry crews would catch fish or go ashore to hunt for fresh meat.

▲ While not in use, the sails were stored away from sea spray in a dry locker, so that they would not rot.

▲ The gunpowder store (magazine) was vital to any pirate ship. The smallest spark could blow it up at any time.

▲ The casks of drinking water weighed a tonne each and also served as ballast, keeping the ship stable. When the casks were empty, the crew went ashore to refill them at fresh springs.

▲ The bilges below decks were full of foul, slopping water. The ship's pumps helped keep the boat dry and afloat.

22

PIRATE SHIPS

Speed and surprise were always the keys to success as a pirate. The buccaneers of the Caribbean soon found out that with small, fast vessels they could easily outwit a slow, lumbering galleon, however heavily it was armed. The French corsairs often used small armed fishing boats to attack English shipping.

Pirates down on their luck might have to use a leaky old tub, but they could always try to capture or steal the very latest in naval design. Many pirate ships were naval or privateering vessels that had been seized by the crew during a mutiny.

Old sailing ships needed constant maintenance and hard work to keep them going. Shipwrecks were common.

▼ The galley was a simple wood-burning range, built for safety well away from the gunpowder store.

► Thick cables called 'forestays' were tied to the bowsprit to support the foremast.

▲ The oars were used when there was no wind, or when the ship was entering a port.

The *Adventure Galley*

This was the ship which took Captain William Kidd on an ill-fated voyage in 1696. It was built the year before on the River Thames at Deptford, near London. The ship was 38 metres long, and was designed for privateering. It was powered by wind and sail, but if the wind failed, the ship could be rowed with 32 oars. Each oar was pulled by two or more men.

Kidd's crew were a bunch of murderous thugs who had been press-ganged into joining up. They forced him to take up piracy. The ship had problems with leaks, and in the end Kidd had to abandon the galley.

► The anchor of the *Adventure Galley* weighed nearly 1,400 kg. Its heavy cable could only be raised with a capstan, which was pushed round and round by the muscle power of the crew. Singing or fiddle music helped the crew to keep the right rhythm and timing.

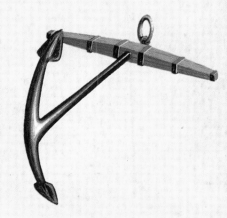

Sails and rigging

The *Adventure Galley* could carry up to 2,675 square metres of sail, which gave it a top speed of about 14 knots (27 kilometres per hour). Sails were made of very tough canvas called 'sailcloth', woven from hemp, cotton or linen. They often had to stand up to gales and hurricanes, so extra sections of sailcloth were stitched on to make the sails tougher.

▼ The *Adventure Galley* was a square-rigged ship. Its square sails were supported by crossbars called yards.

1 sprit topsail
2 spritsail
3 spritsail course
4 inner jib
5 outer jib
6 fore topgallant
7 fore topsail
8 fore top
9 foresail
10 main topgallant
11 main topsail
12 main top
13 mainsail
14 mizzen topgallant
15 mizzen topsail
16 mizzen top
17 spanker
18 yard

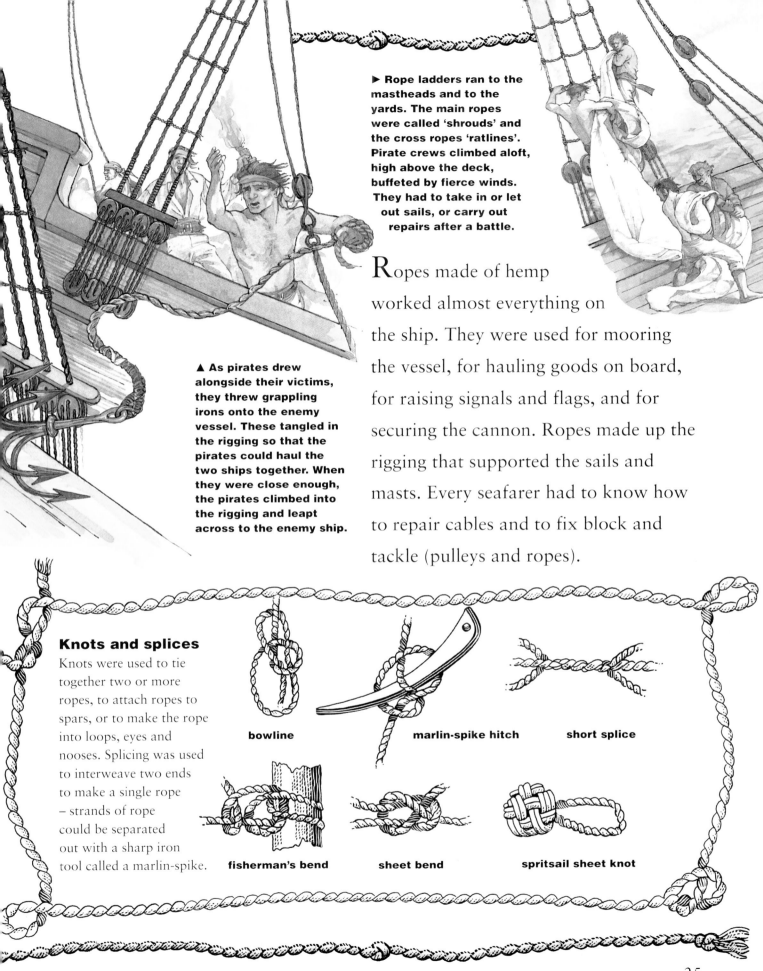

▶ Rope ladders ran to the mastheads and to the yards. The main ropes were called 'shrouds' and the cross ropes 'ratlines'. Pirate crews climbed aloft, high above the deck, buffeted by fierce winds. They had to take in or let out sails, or carry out repairs after a battle.

Ropes made of hemp worked almost everything on the ship. They were used for mooring the vessel, for hauling goods on board, for raising signals and flags, and for securing the cannon. Ropes made up the rigging that supported the sails and masts. Every seafarer had to know how to repair cables and to fix block and tackle (pulleys and ropes).

▲ As pirates drew alongside their victims, they threw grappling irons onto the enemy vessel. These tangled in the rigging so that the pirates could haul the two ships together. When they were close enough, the pirates climbed into the rigging and leapt across to the enemy ship.

Knots and splices

Knots were used to tie together two or more ropes, to attach ropes to spars, or to make the rope into loops, eyes and nooses. Splicing was used to interweave two ends to make a single rope – strands of rope could be separated out with a sharp iron tool called a marlin-spike.

bowline

marlin-spike hitch

short splice

fisherman's bend

sheet bend

spritsail sheet knot

25

Through the ages

The size and design of pirate ships varied greatly from age to age and from one part of the world to another. By the 1800s, sailing ships were faster and more streamlined than ever. This may have helped the pirates, but it also helped the pirate chasers. Soon navies had powerful steamships armed with modern guns to hunt down the pirates.

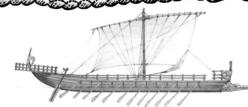

Greek pirate galley, 500 BC
These galleys had oars and a single sail. They were much faster than merchant ships laden with goods.

English nef, 1400
Pirates went into battle on ships with high fighting decks called 'castles' at each end.

English galleon, 1580
Many of Queen Elizabeth I's sea captains engaged in piracy as well as privateering.

Dutch East Indiaman, 1700
Merchant vessels trading with Southeast Asia faced attacks from pirates and privateers.

Galley, 1715
English galleys traded in slaves and sugar in the Americas and were rich prizes for pirates.

Pirate sloop, Nassau, 1720
American sloops were speedy, single-masted ships with a fore-and-aft rig, ideal for the pirates of the Bahamas.

British man-o'-war, 1815
Heavily armed warships like these were used to fight piracy in the Arabian Sea.

Chinese pirate junk, 1845
This three-masted junk was 25 metres long and had a large rudder. It carried 30 cannon.

Paddle-steamer, 1870
Steamships helped the European countries stamp out piracy in Southeast Asia.

Roman pirate chaser, 70 BC
This warship used against Cilician pirates was a trireme, a galley with three banks of oars.

Viking longship, AD 900
Simple but deadly, the longship carried a crew of up to 50 men. It had long oars and a single sail.

Arab dhow, AD 900
This classic ship design is still in use today. The triangular sail is called a 'lateen'.

Spanish galleon, 1580
This heavily-armed Spanish treasure ship was rather clumsy in battle.

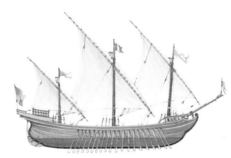

Barbary corsair, 1660
These Muslim galleys from North Africa were rowed by captured Christians who were slaves.

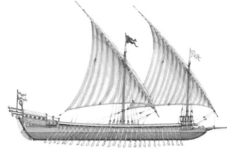

Maltese corsair, 1660
Galleys from Malta attacked the Barbary corsairs. They were rowed by Muslim slaves.

Note: These pirate ships, privateers, merchant vessels and pirate chasers are not shown to scale.

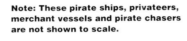

Topsail schooner, 1812
American privateers used these beautiful two-masted vessels to raid British shipping.

British gunship, 1900
By the 1900s few pirates could challenge the power of modern gunship patrols.

Steel and steam replaced wood and sail and, with the coming of radio, few remote islands or lonely coasts were beyond the reach of the law.

Bartholomew Roberts ('Black Bart')

Christopher Moody

Edward Teach ('Blackbeard')

Henry Avery ('Long Ben')

John Rackham ('Calico Jack')

Thomas Tew

Christopher Condent

Pirate flags were meant to strike fear into the enemy. They often showed skulls, swords, crossbones, devils and hearts.

Blackjacks and spyglasses

The first pirate flags were blood red. They were hoisted before battle to signal that no one would be spared. It is thought that the French words *joli rouge* ('pretty red') became the 'Jolly Roger' – the English term for any pirate flag. In the 1690s and 1700s, many pirate captains designed their own flags. They were white on a field of red or, more often, black. These came to be known as 'blackjacks'.

▲ **This beautiful flag was captured from Chinese pirates in 1849. They believed it brought good luck and calm seas.**

Chinese pirate fleets were divided into battle groups. Each one flew under a different coloured flag.

Pirates had to keep a lookout for other vessels all the time. One pirate would climb the main top to look for distant sails on the horizon. The captain would shout out orders to the crew on the quarterdeck if the ship's course had to be changed. The Welsh pirate Howell Davis often used flags to fool his enemies. He flew an English or French flag, or forced vessels he had just defeated to fly a length of black cloth – so that pursuing ships thought they faced a large pirate fleet.

chart

compass

backstaff

dividers

telescope

Finding the way

Navigation is the science of finding the way at sea. A ship's compass has a needle which swings to the north and shows what direction the ship is sailing in. Charts show coastlines, sandbanks, currents and tides. Dividers are used to measure distances on a chart. With a telescope, or 'spyglass', a sailor can identify another ship's flag or sight land.

▼ **This pirate holds the ship on course, turning the wheel to move the rudder. He checks the compass mounted in front of the wheel.**

▼ **His shipmate spies the flag of an enemy through the telescope.**

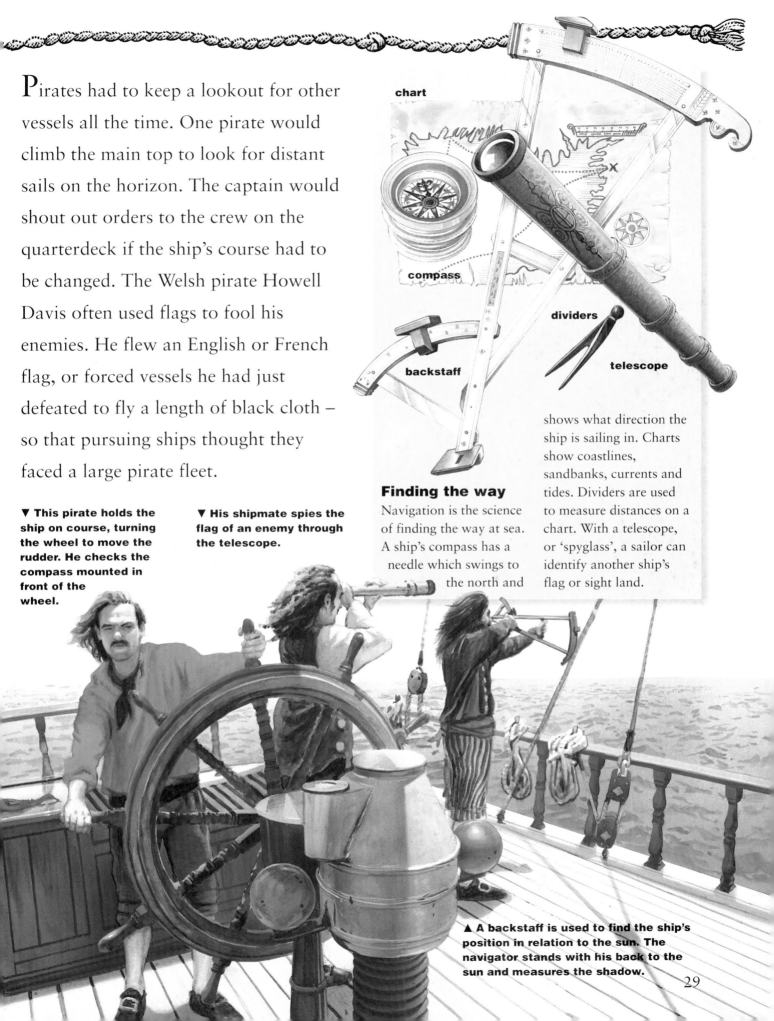

▲ **A backstaff is used to find the ship's position in relation to the sun. The navigator stands with his back to the sun and measures the shadow.**

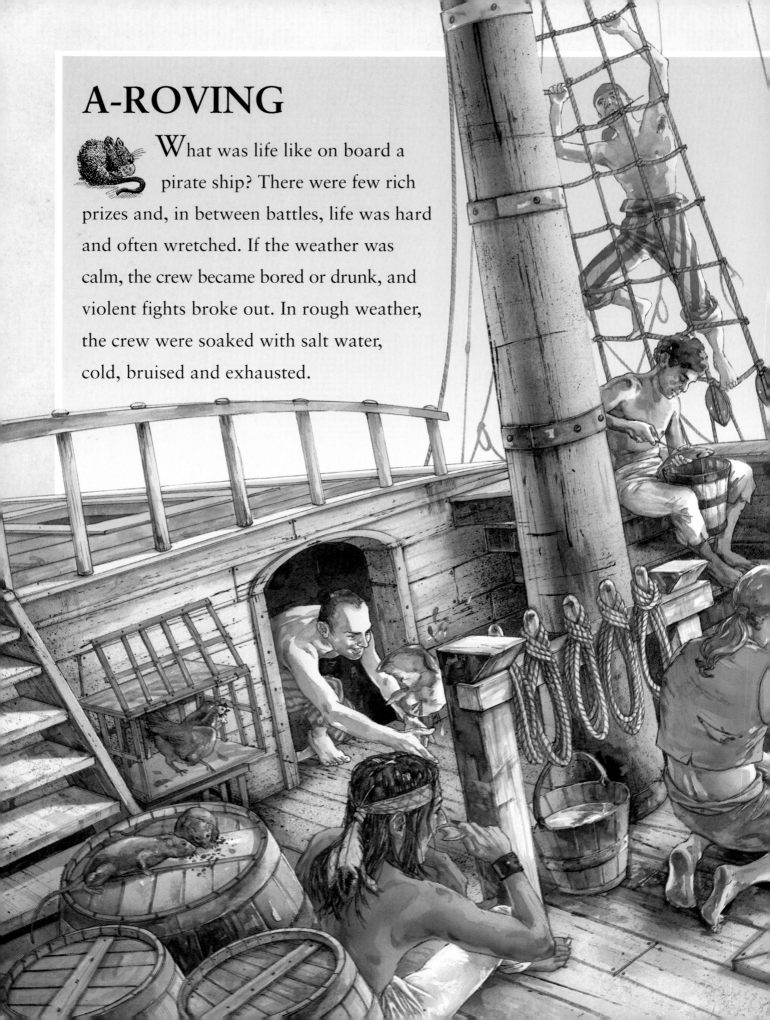

A-ROVING

What was life like on board a pirate ship? There were few rich prizes and, in between battles, life was hard and often wretched. If the weather was calm, the crew became bored or drunk, and violent fights broke out. In rough weather, the crew were soaked with salt water, cold, bruised and exhausted.

▼ These pirates are on the main deck by the galley. One pirate relaxes with a pipe, while another gnaws on 'hard tack', the ship's biscuits that were eaten on most long voyages. The biscuits were nearly always stale and full of wriggling weevils. Meat was dried or salted and in short supply. Chickens were kept on board for their eggs and fish and turtles could be caught over the side of the ship. There were often periods when supplies of fresh water were low. Shipwreck could lead to starvation or even cannibalism among the survivors.

Ship's records

Many old documents show how pirates lived. These accounts on the left list the supplies sold to one ship – from 26 barrels of beer at 60 pieces-of-eight each, to three hats at ten pieces-of-eight. Logbooks were kept by the captain to record every detail of the voyage. They took their name from a piece of wood lowered into the water on a line in order to measure the ship's speed.

At night the pirates who were not on watch slept on the cramped lower decks. This was a dark, closed world, creaking, pitching and tossing. Bilge-water slopped below and rats were everywhere – Chinese pirates liked to eat them. By day the tropical sun could scorch the skin. If pirates were ill, there were no medicines. Limbs injured in battle were sawn off without any anaesthetic, often by the ship's carpenter. For most pirates, the only pleasures were gambling with dice or drinking rum.

▶ Pirates ate little fresh fruit or vegetables at sea and often suffered from scurvy. In 1753 James Lind discovered that eating fruit such as limes could prevent the disease. The explorer Captain Cook was the first to take Lind's advice and included limes in his crew's diet.

'On the account'

Becoming a pirate was called 'going on the account'. Piracy was big business. It may have been criminal and violent, but it was also very organized. Contracts were drawn up between backers and pirate captains. The crews worked out how to divide the spoils and behaved by strict rules. Breaking them could mean a flogging, or even death.

▲ Privateer captains like William Kidd were issued with official documents called 'letters of marque'. These set out the terms for attacking enemy shipping without being accused of piracy.

◄ A wealthy merchant draws up a secret agreement with a pirate captain in a New York tavern. The expenses of a pirate expedition were high, but the rewards could be great.

► A pirate who broke the rules faced severe penalties from his shipmates. He was sometimes 'marooned', or abandoned on a remote desert island. He was left with fresh water, some weapons and gunpowder.

Insurance claims

Just as pirates agreed to obey their captain and follow the rules, the captain and any backers of the expedition were expected to pay pirates for any injuries they received in battle. A finger or eye lost in a sword fight might be worth a compensation award of 100 silver pieces. A whole limb shot away by cannon might be worth 600 silver pieces.

Rules and agreements were drawn up throughout the history of piracy. Pirate crews often voted on which course of action to follow. They saw themselves as free men, making their own decisions in a way that regular sailors could not.

The pirates often made very harsh decisions. If they captured a naval officer under whom they had served, they would treat him with great cruelty. 'Walking the plank', often referred to in storybooks, was not a common punishment, but prisoners were often tortured or killed and thrown to the sharks.

Fighting dirty

Stolen weapons were as valuable as any treasure to a pirate crew. The buccaneers of the Caribbean liked to swagger around with cutlasses and pistols. They used them against one another as much as against the enemy. Blackbeard once shot his first mate, Israel Hands, under the table and smashed his knee-cap. As outlaws, pirates had nothing to lose by fighting to the death. When Blackbeard was finally cornered, it took five shots and 20 cutlass wounds to kill him.

Fire and smoke

In ancient Asia and Europe a blazing mixture of oil and tar was squirted at enemy ships. It was known as 'Greek fire'. The Chinese invented gunpowder about 1,000 years ago, and by the 1300s it was being used to fire primitive cannon. These often blew up, killing the gunners instead of the enemy. The cannon used by the pirates of the 1600s and 1700s were much more reliable. Pirates also made their own fire-bombs and hand grenades.

Cut-throat weapons

Throughout history, pirates simply used whatever weapons they could lay their hands on. The Channel pirates of the Middle Ages might go into battle with boat-hooks and simple knives. A gentleman pirate of the 1720s might have a set of the finest pistols. The most famous pirate weapon was the cutlass. It was a simple short-bladed slashing sword of razor-sharp steel.

French dagger, 1410

musket, 1700

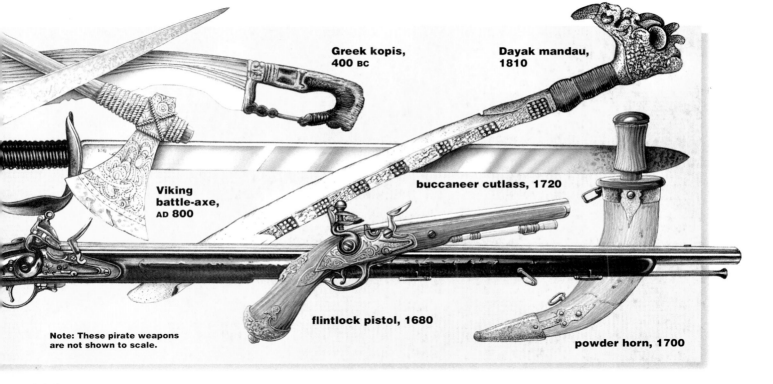

Greek kopis,
400 BC

Dayak mandau,
1810

Viking
battle-axe,
AD 800

buccaneer cutlass, 1720

flintlock pistol, 1680

powder horn, 1700

Note: These pirate weapons
are not shown to scale.

◄ Large cannon were mounted on wheeled bases. The charge of gunpowder was rammed down the barrel. The shot was then loaded and the fuse was lit. When the gun fired, it recoiled backwards with great force, held by ropes. When the shot hit the enemy vessel, it brought masts and spars crashing down and sent splinters flying in all directions.

Many of the rules drawn up by pirate crews referred to personal weapons. The pirates were expected to keep their arms in working order, ready for action at all times. That meant keeping muskets cleaned and gunpowder dry, even when fighting in rough seas or tropical storms.

The long-barrelled muskets and pistols used by the buccaneer sharp-shooters in the 1660s were unreliable, hard to aim and slow to reload. As the fight closed in, the pirates fought hand-to-hand, with cutlasses, daggers and axes. They lashed out violently, kicking, punching and biting.

Pirate treasure

What did pirates dream about? Gold and silver was desired by them all, from the Cilicians of the Mediterranean to the Elizabethan rovers on the Spanish Main. It might take the form of bars, plate, goblets or church crosses, or it might be made into coins. Precious metals, jewellery and fancy weapons could be easily transported and sold. Cargoes such as sugar or tobacco also found a ready market. Spices from the hold of a Dutch East Indiaman were valuable, but had to be dumped if no buyer could be found.

▲ Pirate crews shared out the booty, as agreed in their contract. The spoils could add up to £150,000 or more – many millions at today's values.

Some captains tried to cheat their crew by sailing off before the treasure could be shared out.

► There are few records of buried treasure or secret maps. Pirates may have come ashore by night to hide their treasure on remote islands. They may also have used the old smugglers' trick of anchoring barrels of contraband to the seabed by weighting them with stones.

Pieces-of-eight

Coins minted on the Spanish Main were sent back to Europe with the treasure fleets. They included doubloons and eight-reale pieces.

Reale is Spanish for 'royal', but the buccaneers called them 'pieces-of-eight'. These types of coin stayed in use in the Caribbean for many years.

In a raid, pirates took anything they could use, including weapons, tools, medical chests, flags, ropes and sails. They often took the whole ship, forcing its crew to join theirs. Ships that were of no use might be sunk or 'scuttled'. This was done by a privateer's first mate called David Jones, in the 1630s. From then on, anything sent to the seabed was said to be 'sent to Davy Jones's locker'.

Hidden hoards

Treasure hunters may never have found chests full of gold hidden *by* pirates, but they have often found hoards hidden *from* pirates. Wealthy Romans in Britain hid their valuables from Saxon pirates. Monks buried church treasure in case the Vikings got hold of it. On the Spanish Main, priests covered a gold altar in white paint – so that Morgan's buccaneers would think it was wood.

A pirate's death

Few pirates lived to enjoy their wealth. Some, like the English corsair Sir Henry Mainwaring, gained a royal pardon and abandoned piracy. Most pirates died in distant lands, in brutal battles. Thomas Tew was shot during an attack on the Mogul ship *Fateh Muhammad* in 1695. Thomas Anstis was killed in the Caribbean in about 1723, murdered by his own crew. John Ward, who turned Barbary corsair under the name 'Yusuf Raïs', died of plague in Tunis in 1622. The ones who made it home, like Henry Avery, often died penniless and forgotten.

Death of William Marsh

William de Marisco, or Marsh, was a pirate based on the island of Lundy, in the Bristol Channel. He was captured in 1242 and taken to London. There he was hauled through the streets, hanged, quartered (chopped into four pieces) and burned.

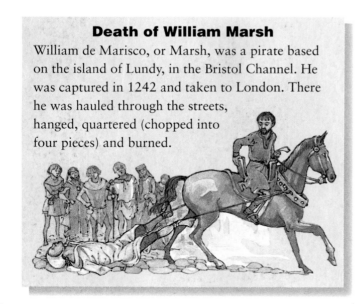

▶ Large crowds turned out to watch pirates being hanged at Execution Dock by the River Thames. Their bodies were placed in iron cages so that no one could steal the bones and bury them. Kidd's tarred body swung from a gibbet in 1701.

▲ Everyone wanted to read reports of the trial of John Rackham (Calico Jack), Anne Bonny and Mary Read. In the 1700s, popular songs were written about such pirates and their evil deeds.

From earliest times, laws against piracy were savage. Captured pirates were tortured and enslaved. The Romans nailed pirates to crosses. The German pirate Störtebeker had his head cut off in Hamburg in 1402. English pirates of the 1700s were hanged at Execution Dock in London. The tide was allowed to wash over their bodies, which were then tarred and hung in chains as a warning to all – piracy never pays.

CHANGING TIMES

The European pirates who terrorized the oceans between the 1500s and the 1800s were fighting at a time when Europe was trying to control the rest of the world and build up big empires overseas. Some pirates preyed off the new empires. Others, such as Henry Morgan, helped to create them.

▼ On November 13, 1809, the pirate base at Ra's al Khayma, on the Persian Gulf, was destroyed by a British task-force. Piracy was soon under threat around the world.

▲ These captured Chinese pirates were photographed on board a British naval patrol vessel. The fight against pirates in the South China Sea lasted from the 1840s until the 1920s.

By the mid-1800s this long period of piracy was coming to an end. Britain and several other European nations now ruled most of the world. They controlled trade and they had the most powerful guns and ships. The bombardment of Algiers in 1816 marked the end of the Barbary pirates' power in the Mediterranean. Slavery was gradually stamped out. Dutch warships patrolled Southeast Asia, and the British attacked the pirates of the South China Sea.

▶ In 1840 a British explorer called James Brooke became the rajah, or ruler, of Sarawak, on the island of Borneo. He organized a series of devastating attacks on the Dayak pirates.

Rogues' gallery

Alwilda
(active fifth century AD)
This princess from Gotland, Sweden, is said to have turned pirate when her father tried to force her into marriage. She changed her mind about her husband-to-be when he captured her during a sea battle.

Kanhoji Angria (died 1729)
Kanhoji Angria was the first of his family to lead attacks on British shipping off the west coast of India in the 1700s.

Henry Avery ('Long Ben')
(1685–c. 1728)
Avery was the 'Arch-Pirate', an Englishman who became famous for his brutal and highly profitable attack on the Mogul ship *Gang-i-Sawai* in the Arabian Sea.

Aruj Barbarossa (died 1518) and Kheir-ed-din Barbarossa (died 1546)
The Greek-born Barbarossa ('red-beard') brothers founded the power of the Barbary corsairs in the 1500s, attacking Christian shipping and coastal towns around the Mediterranean.

Jean Bart (1651–1702)
This fisherman's son from Dunkirk raided North Sea and English Channel fleets. He served in the Dutch navy and later became a successful privateer for the French. He made a famous escape in a small boat from Plymouth, in Devon.

Bartolomeo 'el Portugués'
(active 1660s–1670s)
Famous for his lucky escapes, this Portuguese buccaneer was one of the first to be based in Jamaica. His luck finally ran out in a shipwreck.

Sam 'Black' Bellamy
(active 1715–1717)
Devon-born Sam Bellamy travelled to Cape Cod, North America, in about 1715. He went to Florida in search of Spanish treasure and turned pirate. He captured the *Whydah* in 1717, but died when it sank in a fierce storm.

Stede Bonnet (died 1718)
Bonnet was a respectable middle-aged man who suddenly took up a life of crime. Blackbeard found his dress and manner hugely amusing. Bonnet was hanged at Charleston harbour in North America in 1718.

Anne Bonny (active 1719)
This Irishwoman left her husband for 'Calico Jack' Rackham in the Bahamas. Women were banned from most pirate vessels in the 1700s, but she became one of the most famous fighters of her day. When Rackham was hanged in Jamaica, Bonny was pardoned because she was pregnant.

Roche Brasiliano
(active 1670s)
This Dutch buccaneer lived in Brazil before turning up in Jamaica in the 1670s. A drunkard famous for his cruelty, he was elected pirate captain and terrorized Spanish shipping.

Nicholas Brown (died 1726)
Known as the 'Grand Pirate', Brown was once given a royal pardon but went back to attacking shipping off Jamaica. He was captured by a childhood friend, John Drudge. When Brown died of his wounds, Drudge cut off his head and pickled it, so that he could claim a reward.

Madame Cheng
(active 1807–1810)
This ruthless woman took over her husband's pirate fleet when he died and turned it into a huge organization. She was famous throughout the South China Sea for her cruelty.

Christopher Condent
(active 1718–1720)
This savage pirate came from Plymouth in Devon. In the Bahamas, he took to the Pirate Round and attacked merchant ships off Africa and Arabia. He settled in Madagascar and Mauritius before retiring to St Malo in France.

Cui Apu (died 1851)
This Chinese pirate commanded a fleet of over 500 junks in the South China Sea during the 1800s. His activities were put to an end by British warships.

William Dampier
(1652–1715)
William Dampier came from Somerset and fought alongside buccaneers in

Central Amercia. Marooned on the Nicobar Islands in the Indian Ocean, he escaped in a canoe and wrote about his travels in *Voyage around the World* (1697). Dampier was a brilliant navigator and later explored the waters around Australia.

Simon Danziger or Dansker (Dali Raïs or 'Captain Devil') (died 1611)

This Dutch privateer sailed out of Marseilles in southern France in the 1600s, but took up service with the Barbary corsairs. He captured many Christian ships and taught the Muslims seafaring skills required for the North Atlantic waters. Danziger then changed sides again – only to be seized and hanged in Tunis.

Howell Davis (active 1719)

A Welsh pirate, Davis attacked slaving ships off Africa's Guinea Coast. He was killed in an ambush at the Portuguese colony of Principe.

Francis Drake (*c.* 1540–1596)

Drake was a great English seaman and explorer. In 1578–1580, he sailed around the world in the *Golden Hind*, engaged in piracy and privateering, and was knighted by Queen Elizabeth I on his return.

Réné Duguay-Trouin (1673–1736)

This Breton corsair from St Malo became so famous for his attacks on British shipping that he was made a French naval commander and was given many public honours.

Peter Easton (active 1607–1612)

Easton was an English pirate who commanded 17 ships and carried out attacks from Newfoundland to West Africa. Having won a fortune, he settled in the south of France and was made a marquis.

Edward England (died *c.* 1720)

Edward England may in fact have been an Irishman named Jasper Seager. He sailed with Bartholomew Roberts on the Guinea Coast, but was later marooned in Mauritius.

Eustace 'the Black Monk' (active 1200s)

This Flemish-born monk turned outlaw and raided shipping in the English Channel. He was said to have a pact with the devil and the power to make his ship invisible. But he was defeated in a sea battle in 1217 and had his head cut off.

John Evans (active 1720s)

Captain John Evans was a Welsh sailor who ended up in Port Royal, Jamaica. In 1722, he and his shipmates raided the Jamaican coast from a piragua and captured many ships. Evans was shot in a quarrel with his bosun off Grand Cayman.

Alexandre Exquemelin (active 1660s–1690s)

Probably born in Normandy, France, Exquemelin was a surgeon who went to the Caribbean with the French West India Company and joined the Tortuga buccaneers. Back in Europe he wrote the famous *Bucaniers of America* (1678), and then returned to the Spanish Main in the 1690s.

Jean Fleury or Florin (died 1527)

One of the first French corsairs to attack a Spanish treasure fleet, Fleury was a privateer in the service of the Viscount of Dieppe.

Antonio Fuët (active 1660s–1690s)

This French pirate from Narbonne was known as 'Captain Moidore'. Once, when he was attacking a ship, Fuët ran out of shot and had to load up his cannon with *moidores* – these were a type of gold coin used in Portugal and Brazil.

Klein Hänslein ('Little Jack') (died 1573)

This German pirate of the 1570s attacked shipping in the North Sea until he and his crew were captured and beheaded in Hamburg.

Sir John Hawkins (1532–1595)

A privateer from Plymouth in Devon, Hawkins was one of the first traders to ship slaves from West Africa to the Caribbean.

Victor Hugues (active 1790s)

Born in Marseilles, this Frenchman lost his business in Haiti when the slaves there demanded freedom. So he turned to piracy and made a fortune by raiding shipping out of Guadeloupe.

Jan Jansz (Murad Raïs) (active 1620s)

This Dutch privateer joined the Barbary corsairs and in 1627 led a Muslim fleet to Iceland, where they took slaves and plunder.

John Paul Jones (1747–1792)

Scottish-born Jones became an American hero in the war of independence – he attacked ships in British waters and was condemned as a traitor and pirate. Later a rear-admiral in the Russian navy, he died in France.

William Kidd (c. 1645–1701)

Kidd was a Scottish sea captain who lived in New York City. He was commissioned as a privateer, but took up piracy in the Indian Ocean and was hanged at London in 1701.

Lady Mary Killigrew (active 1580s)

The Killigrew family were secret backers of piracy in Cornwall. In 1583 a Spanish merchant ship was driven into Falmouth by storms. Lady Killigrew led a boarding party onto the vessel, killing the crew and stealing the cargo. She was sentenced to death for piracy, but was let off.

Jean Lafitte (active 1810s)

This French pirate attacked ships in the Caribbean and Indian Ocean. He became a big gangster in New Orleans, but was hailed as an all-American hero after defending the city against the British in 1812.

François le Clerc (active 1553–1554)

This French privateer was known as Jambe de Bois ('pegleg') because of his wooden leg. He attacked Spanish ships off Puerto Rico and Hispaniola, and sacked the port of Santiago de Cuba with eight ships and 300 men.

François l'Ollonois (Jean-David Nau) (active 1660s)

Born in Sables d'Olonne, France, Nau became one of the cruellest of all the buccaneers. He took part in many horrible attacks on the Spanish Main, but was himself captured by Native American warriors, hacked to bits and burned over a fire.

George Lowther (active 1720s)

Lowther sailed to West Africa as second mate on a merchant ship called the *Gambia Castle*, joined up with some soldiers on board and seized the vessel, changing its name to the *Delivery*. He took up piracy along the coasts of the Caribbean and North America. In 1728 his pirates were careening their ship when they came under attack. Lowther is thought to have shot himself, and some of his crew were arrested and hanged.

Henry Mainwaring (1587–1653)

This English knight was a pirate hunter who ended up turning to piracy himself. He was based in Morocco from 1612, and spent four years attacking merchant shipping in the Mediterranean. Then he returned to England and received a pardon.

William Marsh or de Marisco (died 1242)

A violent enemy of King Henry III of England, Marsh based himself on Lundy Island in the Bristol Channel. From there he raided ships in the Irish Sea and demanded ransoms for his captives.

Henry Morgan (c. 1635–1688)

In his youth, this Welsh buccaneer was kidnapped at the port of Bristol and shipped to Barbados. In the Caribbean he became the most famous organizer of buccaneer armies against the Spanish, carrying out raids with military precision, but without mercy. He was honoured by the British authorities in Jamaica before dying of drink.

Grace O' Malley (active 1560s–1580s)

This Irish noblewoman led attacks on shipping off the west coast of Ireland. In 1593 she won a pardon and a pension from Queen Elizabeth I. She then retired, handing over her business to her sons.

James Plantain (active 1720s)

Born in Jamaica, this pirate set up his base on Madgascar. He built a fortress at Ranter Bay and declared himself 'king'. He kept many wives and was said to live in luxury.

John Rackham ('Calico Jack') (died 1720)

John Rackham and Anne Bonny set up in partnership in the Bahamas in 1719. Rackham was hanged in Jamaica in 1720. "If he had fought like a man," said Anne, "he need not have been hanged like a dog."

Raga (active 1820s)

Chief of the Malay pirates in the Straits of Makassar, Raga took many European ships and beheaded their crews. His base at Kuala Batu, Sumatra, was destroyed by an American task force.

Rahmah bin Jabr

(c. 1756–1826)
The most famous pirate of the Persian Gulf, this one-eyed captain plundered shipping for 50 years. At the age of 70, in battle with the whole fleet of Bahrain, he set fire to the gunpowder magazine on his own dhow, blowing half the enemy (and himself) sky high.

Sir Walter Raleigh

(1552–1618)
An Elizabethan courtier and navigator, Raleigh fitted out many privateering expeditions in order to fund a new colony in Virginia, North America. On the death of Queen Elizabeth I, Raleigh's fortunes changed. In 1616 he persuaded James I to send him on another search for gold, but he returned empty-handed and was beheaded.

Mary Read (active 1719–1721)

This Englishwoman, who often dressed as a man, fought as a soldier in Flanders and owned a tavern before sailing to the Caribbean. When her ship was captured by Rackham and Bonny, she joined their crew. Like Bonny, Read escaped the gallows because she was expecting a baby. She died of fever in Jamaica in 1721.

Basil Ringrose (c. 1653–1686)

This English surgeon travelled through Panama with Bartholomew Sharp and his buccaneers in 1680–1682, and wrote about his travels. He was killed in Mexico.

Bartholomew Roberts ('Black Bart') (1682–1722)

A Welsh pirate captain, Roberts is said to have seized 400 ships off West Africa and in the Caribbean. His biggest coup was capturing the *Sagrada Familia*, a Portuguese vessel carrying a fortune in coins, diamonds and goods from Brazil.

Abraham Samuel

(active 1690s)
Of mixed African and European descent, Jamaican Abraham Samuel proclaimed himself pirate 'king' of Port Dauphin, on Madagascar, in the days of the Pirate Round.

Richard Sawkins (died 1680)

Buccaneer captain in the Caribbean, Sawkins attacked Spanish shipping and outwitted the British navy. He fought in Panama and was killed there at Pueblo Nuevo.

Störtebeker (active 1390s)

This former merchant formed a pirate band called 'The Friends of God and Enemies of the World'. They sailed the Baltic Sea and attacked the city of Bergen, in Norway. He was executed in 1402.

Robert Surcouf (1773–1827)

Originally from the corsair haven of St Malo, this famous privateer attacked British shipping in the Indian Ocean with devastating success. He captured the *Triton* in 1795 and the *Kent* in 1800.

Sweyn Forkbeard (died 1014)

Viking King of Denmark, Sweyn defeated and killed his own father, Harald Bluetooth. He led many piratical raids against England, receiving huge sums of money in payment of ransom demands.

Edward Teach or Thatch ('Blackbeard') (died 1718)

A crazy pirate with his beard and long hair tied in plaits, Blackbeard terrorized the North American coast before being killed in battle. His fame soon spread around the world.

Thomas Tew (died 1695)

Born in Rhode Island, Tew commanded a ship called the *Amity* and attacked Mogul shipping in the Indian Ocean. He made a fortune from his first voyage, but was killed on his second.

Charles Vane (died 1720)

When Vane came to New Providence in 1718, he was already known as a boastful, bullying desperado. He terrorized Caribbean shipping but lost his ship in a storm in 1720. He was brought to trial in Spanish Town, Jamaica, and was hanged.

Francis Verney (1584–1615)

This English gentleman 'turned Turk' and went off to become a Barbary corsair at the age of 23. Based at Algiers, Sir Francis attacked English shipping but was captured by a Christian galley and enslaved.

John Ward (Yusuf Raïs)

(c. 1553–1622)
An English sea captain turned Barbary corsair, Ward was based in Tunis, where he died of plague.

EARLY DAYS

American Indians lived undisturbed throughout North and South America until the European discovery of the 'New World' in 1492. Now the nations of Europe raced to claim the rich 'new' land for themselves. But it was the Spanish *conquistadores* (conquerors) who had the greatest impact on the native people.

The king of Spain was determined to find the legendary 'Seven Cities of Gold'. To the Southwest came Francisco Vásquez de Coronado and to the East, Hernando de Soto. Despite vast armies of men and animals, neither man found the mythical treasure.

The Spanish treated the Pueblo Indians of New Mexico very harshly. In 1680 the Indians fought back, killing almost 400 Spaniards and stealing their horses. Until then, dogs were used to carry heavy loads but now horses, called 'big dogs', took their place. Within one hundred years, most tribes had horses. On horseback, they could hunt farther afield.

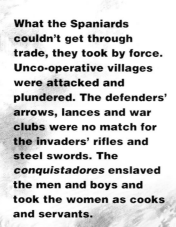

What the Spaniards couldn't get through trade, they took by force. Unco-operative villages were attacked and plundered. The defenders' arrows, lances and war clubs were no match for the invaders' rifles and steel swords. The *conquistadores* enslaved the men and boys and took the women as cooks and servants.

▼ In 1783, colonists in the East declared their independence from Britain, and the United States was formed. But up until the early 1800s, vast areas of the continent remained colonies, belonging to Spain, France and Britain. Gradually, the United States started to expand its boundaries. Sometimes it fought for territory, as it did with Britain in 1812. It also bought land. In 1803, Napoleon sold Louisiana to the United States for $15 million.

BRITISH (until 1818)

FRENCH (The Louisiana Purchase 1803)

SPANISH (Mexican after 1823)

THE UNITED STATES 1783

N

MILES 500
KM 800

KEY TO STATES WITH DATES THEY JOINED THE UNION
1 Michigan 1837
2 Illinois 1818
3 Indiana 1816
4 Ohio 1803
5 Vermont 1791
6 Maine 1820
7 Missouri 1821
8 Kentucky 1792
9 Arkansas 1836
10 Tennessee 1796
11 Louisiana 1812
12 Mississippi 1817
13 Alabama 1819
14 Florida 1819

The wild frontier

In 1803, President Jefferson bought the Louisiana Territory from France. The land stretched all the way from the Mississippi River to the eastern slopes of the Rocky Mountains. Expeditions set out to map the West. Many of the early explorers, such as Zebulon Pike, Jim Bridger and Thomas 'Brokenhand' Fitzpatrick, became the first settlers of the wild frontier, trapping furs in the mountains for their living. The West captured the imagination as a place of opportunity, freedom and rich land; the rush to settle the West had begun.

Early explorers

Meriwether Lewis and William Clark captained the president's Corps of Discovery – the expedition to explore the new territory and reach the Pacific coast. They took three boats laden with gifts and trading goods, and 30 men. Clark brought along his black slave, York. They also hired a young Shoshoni woman, called Sacajawea, to be their guide. The expedition took over a year, crossing the Rockies along the Oregon Trail, and reaching the coast in 1805.

Mountain man of legend

James 'Tomahawk' Beckwourth headed west from Virginia in 1826. There, he met a Crow woman who claimed he was her long lost son, and called him Morning Star. The tribe adopted him and he fought alongside Crow warriors against the Blackfeet. He became a war chief and he was even married to a chief's two daughters at the same time. He later worked as a government guide and interpreter. He found a route through the Sierra Nevada Mountains to California, and it was named the Beckwourth Pass after him.

▶ *Fall of the Alamo,* by Robert Onderdonk

▲ In the early 1830s Texas was under Mexican control. A small Spanish mission and fortress called The Alamo was the site of a bloody 12-day siege in 1836. All 182 Texan defenders, including the famous Davy Crockett, Jim Bowie and Colonel William Travis, were massacred by 3,000 Mexican troops. But just six weeks later, Texas finally won its independence with the stirring battle cry of 'Remember the Alamo!'. In 1845 Texas joined the Union and became the 28th American state. This new land continued the westward expansion of American control. And because of the large herds of cattle there, Texas was settled by ranchers and cowboys and became a vital part of the West's cattle industry.

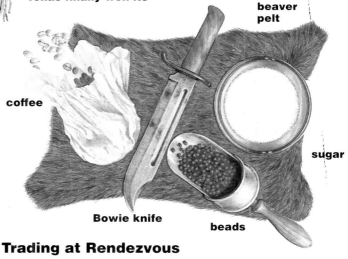

beaver pelt

coffee

sugar

Bowie knife

beads

Trading at Rendezvous

After lonely trapping in the wilds, the highlight of a mountain man's year was the month-long meeting called Rendezvous. He traded his furs for knives, sugar and gunpowder. But best of all there was plenty of whiskey, gambling and horse-racing!

Clues to the past

The true days of the Wild West began with the Louisiana Purchase in 1803 and came to an end in 1890. Paintings, photographs, diaries, letters, newspapers and American Indian artefacts surviving from that time allow historians to build up a picture of how the people of the West lived – and died.

▶ *The Cowboy*, by Frederic Remington

◀ If you couldn't write down words, how would you keep a record of your family history or honour a dead chief? Totem poles are found mainly in the far Northwest of the United States. Some tell of a tribe's ancestors; 'shame poles' were built to disgrace people; others were like upright coffins, containing a dead body. Like this Kwakiutl totem pole, many still stand today and they tell us a lot about the way of life of the American Indians who carved and painted them.

AMERICAN INDIAN ARTEFACTS
1 Ice Age stone weapon point, found at Folsom, New Mexico
2 Chipewyan caribou bone scraper
3 Papago pot
4 Ute moccasins
5 Potawatomi pipe
6 Pima coiled basket
7 Naiche painting on doeskin
8 Navajo blanket
9 Iroquois carved antler comb

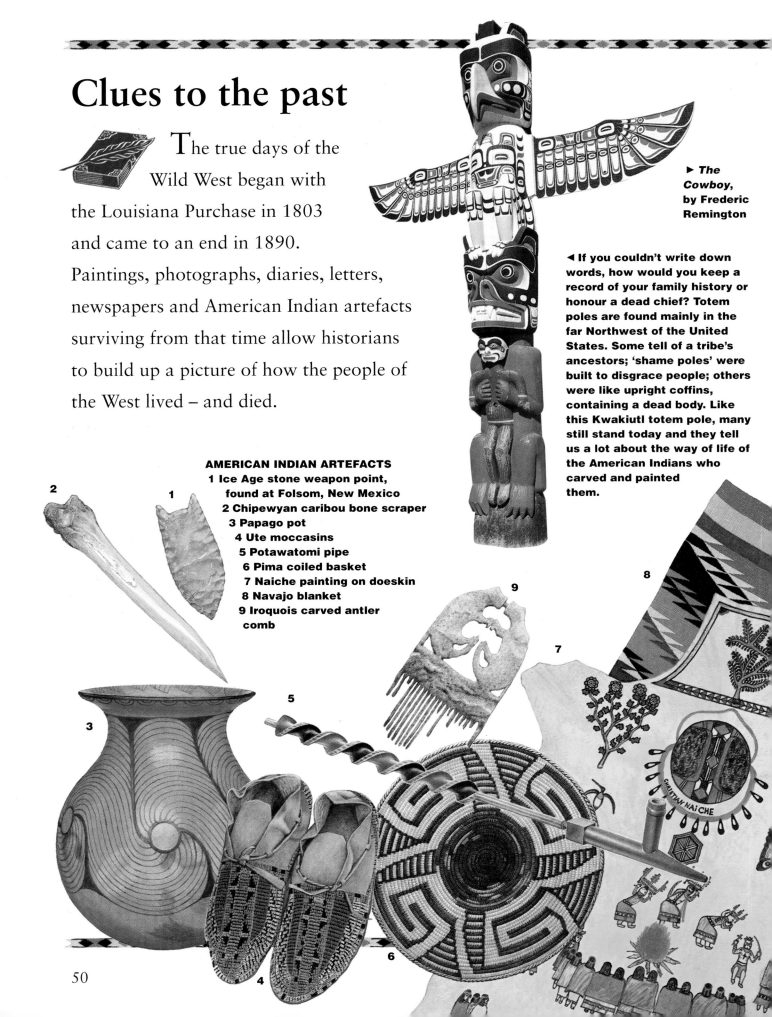

Photography

The first photograph was taken in 1826 and the time of the Wild West is one of the earliest in history to be recorded by photos. Pictures have survived of everything, from the unspoilt landscapes to the characters who lived there – cowboys, settlers, gold-miners and American Indians.

On canvas

Painters George Catlin, Karl Bodmer, Mary Foote and Albert Bierstadt knew that they had to capture the Wild West before it vanished forever. Frederic Remington and Charles Russell rode alongside cowboys and soldiers, recording what they saw in beautiful paintings.

▼ Using wool from their own sheep, Navajo women wove these colourful, patterned blankets so tight that they were almost waterproof. Even the smallest took weeks to complete.

The written word

Ordinary diaries, like that of Susan Shelby Magoffin, were simple accounts of everyday experiences. Many early settlers wrote private diaries which were later published. Accounts of frontier life by famous explorers sold in huge numbers at the time, to readers eager for excitement. Guidebooks are also a valuable source of first-hand information; they were written to let a settler know what to expect and to describe the conditions on a wagon train.

Susan Shelby Magoffin

In a typical Dakota (or Sioux) village on the plains, a stream provided water, cottonwood trees supplied firewood, young spring grass fed the horses and there was plenty of open space to pitch the tepees.

It took up to 12 buffalo hides to make a family tepee. It was the women who made, owned and erected the tepees, stretching the hides over pine poles. A fire inside kept everyone warm in winter, while in summer the sides were lifted to let the breeze in.

Games were enjoyed by old and young alike. Men and boys played stickball, which was known as 'little brother of war' because many ended up with cuts or even broken bones! Horse races were popular, too, and men liked to gamble with stones and straws.

▶ Only the women made clothes. The buffalo skin was pegged out, scraped free of flesh, then washed with water and grease. Once cleaned, the skin was left to dry in the sun. Then the women rubbed it for days until it was soft and pliable.

TEPEE LIFE

Each American Indian tribe had its own way of life, suited to its surroundings. But all tribes had a similar social structure. The three most important men were the chief, the medicine man and the war chief. Next came the elders and warriors, then the squaws and children. Like other Plains Indians, the Dakota (or Sioux) lived in villages. Life was hard. Those children who survived were cared for by all the members of the tribe. They had toys, games and pet puppies. Boys practised with bows and arrows. Dolls were popular with the girls, who learned the skills they'd need for adult life from their mothers.

▲ To make pemmican, cut buffalo meat into narrow strips and dry slowly over a fire or in the sun. Pound this 'jerky' and mix with chokecherries and buffalo fat. Stored in sacks, this food can keep for five years.

► After the chief, the most important man was the medicine man, or shaman. He was the contact between the real world and the spirit world. He cured illnesses with his magic and medicine.

Homes of the brave

With the coming of the horse, it was much easier for American Indians to move about freely. They often moved with the seasons. Some tribes, such as the Arapaho, followed the migrating buffalo. They spent the hot summer months in the cool north and moved south as it grew colder.

Almost half of the North American Indian tribes were based between the Mississippi River and the Rocky Mountains. But tribes were often forced out of their original homelands, either by settlers or by other jealous tribes. The eastern tribes were the first to obtain guns. They used them to push other tribes west and steal their land.

Who lived where?

Tribes are sometimes grouped together by area. The four western areas are the Southwest, Plains, Northwest Coast and California-Intermountain. The other, non-western areas are the Far North, Caribbean, Middle American and Eastern Woodlands.

Western tribes

Frontiersmen and pioneers encountered many different tribes in the Wild West. Each was distinct and usually had its own language. Many tribes named themselves after their holy ancestors. These spiritual guardians were known as the 'totem' and often took the form of an animal.

Tlingit (Northwest Coast)

Hupa (California-Intermountain)

Pawnee (Plains)

Navajo (Southwest)

Types of dwelling

Depending on what building material was to hand, different tribes had different types of houses. Pueblos (1) were built from adobe bricks, tepees (2) from hides, wigwams (3) of bark and leaves, and lodges (4) from earth and wood.

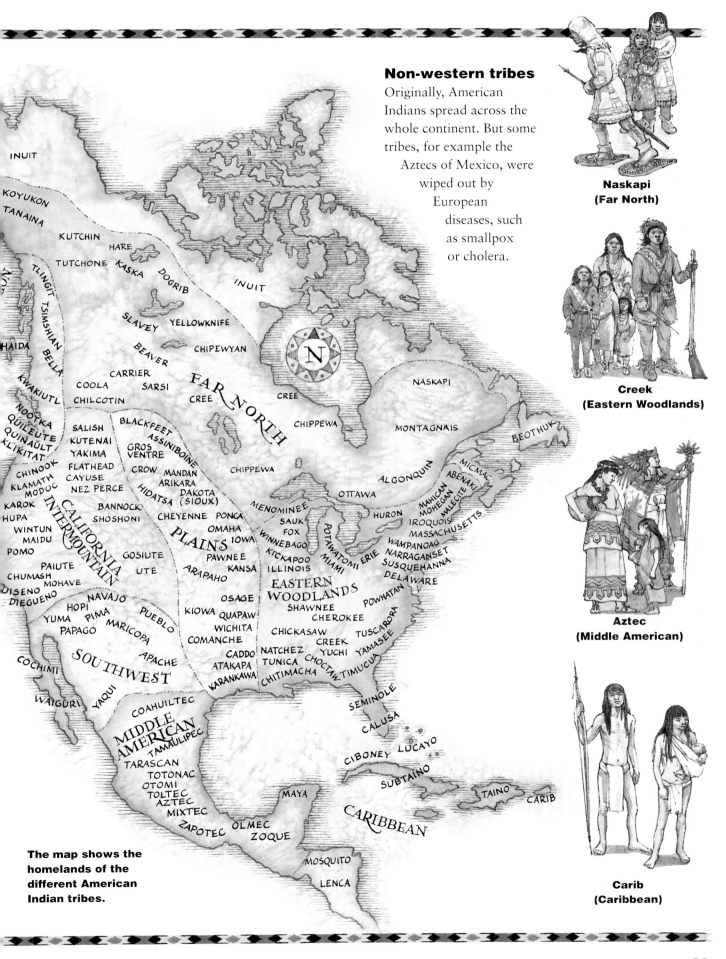

Non-western tribes
Originally, American Indians spread across the whole continent. But some tribes, for example the Aztecs of Mexico, were wiped out by European diseases, such as smallpox or cholera.

Naskapi (Far North)

Creek (Eastern Woodlands)

Aztec (Middle American)

Carib (Caribbean)

INUIT
KOYUKON
TANAINA
KUTCHIN
HARE
TUTCHONE KASKA DOGRIB
INUIT
TLINGIT
TSIMSHIAN SLAVEY YELLOWKNIFE
HAIDA BELLA BEAVER CHIPEWYAN
CARRIER FAR NORTH
KWAKIUTL COOLA SARSI CREE CREE NASKAPI
NOOTKA CHILCOTIN
QUILEUTE SALISH BLACKFEET CHIPPEWA MONTAGNAIS
QUINAULT KUTENAI ASSINIBOINE
KLIKITAT YAKIMA GROS VENTRE BEOTHUK
CHINOOK FLATHEAD CROW MANDAN CHIPPEWA ALGONQUIN MICMAC
KLAMATH CAYUSE ARIKARA ABENAKI
MODOC NEZ PERCE HIDATSA DAKOTA OTTAWA MAHICAN MALECITE
KAROK BANNOCK (SIOUX) MENOMINEE HURON MOHEGAN
HUPA SHOSHONI CHEYENNE PONCA SAUK IROQUOIS MASSACHUSETTS
WINTUN OMAHA FOX WAMPANOAG
MAIDU PLAINS IOWA WINNEBAGO ERIE NARRAGANSET
POMO GOSIUTE PAWNEE KICKAPOO POTAWATOMI SUSQUEHANNA
PAIUTE UTE KANSA MIAMI ILLINOIS DELAWARE
CHUMASH MOHAVE ARAPAHO
DISENO EASTERN POWHATAN
DIEGUENO NAVAJO WOODLANDS
HOPI PUEBLO OSAGE KIOWA QUAPAW SHAWNEE
YUMA PIMA WICHITA CHEROKEE TUSCARORA
PAPAGO MARICOPA COMANCHE CHICKASAW CREEK YAMASEE
APACHE CADDO NATCHEZ YUCHI
COCHIMI SOUTHWEST ATAKAPA TUNICA CHOCTAW TIMUCUA
WAIGURI KARANKAWA CHITIMACHA
YAQUI COAHUILTEC SEMINOLE
MIDDLE CALUSA
AMERICAN
TAMAULIPEC CIBONEY LUCAYO
TARASCAN SUBTAINO
TOTONAC MAYA TAINO
OTOMI CARIB
TOLTEC OLMEC
AZTEC ZAPOTEC ZOQUE CARIBBEAN
MIXTEC
MOSQUITO
LENCA

The map shows the homelands of the different American Indian tribes.

Hunting and food

Some tribes were hunters, relying on buffalo and other game for food, shelter and clothing. Most American Indians gathered foods from the wild, too. Tribes such as the Mandans, who lived in areas of good soil, were excellent farmers. In fact, 60 percent of the crops we grow today come from plants first cultivated by the American Indians. They include corn, beans, tomatoes, squash, potatoes, chilli peppers and vanilla. Not all crops provided food – there were medicinal herbs, tobacco, cotton, and plants for vegetable dyes.

Using the buffalo

Every part of the buffalo was used. The meat fed the family, while soap made from the fat kept them clean. Bones were carved into tools and knives, and the hide made clothing, tepees and shields. Thick buffalo hair was woven into rope or used for children's toys.

BUFFALO PRODUCTS
1 sacred decorated skull
2 toy made of buffalo hair
3 leather war shield
4 pemmican hammer of leather and bone
5 buffalo-skin blanket

The buffalo runners

Before the days of rifles, hunting buffalo was a dangerous business. A hunter would ride in close, select one buffalo, and herd it away from the others. A team of skilled hunters could kill a small herd in about 15 minutes, but if they weren't careful, they could be thrown from their horses and be stampeded to death by the panicking animals.

Preparing the corn

Corn was part of the American Indian's staple diet. Women ground the kernels into flour between two stones. To make corn fritters, water was added to the flour, the cakes were fried in a skillet over the fire.

Tasty harvest

Corn (1), beans and squash (2) were the three main crops and were often called the Trinity. Women grew them in their own gardens. Sunflowers (3) were grown, too, for their nutritious seeds, and rice (4) was gathered from the wild. Vanilla pods and wild berries (5) were used in cooking and preserving.

The wolf headdress shows this warrior is a scout.

A horse's war paint showed how many raids it had made.

coup stick

CHEYENNE WARRIOR

What's your name?

Some children had no name until they were teenagers. Like many, the Apache chief Black Eagle got his through a vision (1). He earned his name by taking part in a horse-stealing raid, where he saw the eagle from his dream (2). Black Eagle went on to become chief of his tribe (3).

Warriors

Not only did tribes fight the settlers and soldiers, they warred amongst themselves to gain new territory and to prove their courage. The Dakota were great enemies of the Crow and Pawnees. The Comanche were swift and ferocious on horseback, and everyone feared the Apaches. Eagle-feather headdresses, known as 'war bonnets', were worn only by those who earned them by their acts of bravery. Others wore simple headbands or skullcaps.

◄ Warriors would kill or even scalp the enemy, but one of the most respected war deeds was 'counting coup' – touching the enemy but not killing him. The more coups counted, the greater a man's status as a warrior. Many used a special, curved stick, called a coup stick, which was decorated with eagle feathers.

58

3

2

Dressed to kill

In addition to their headdresses, which showed their position within their tribe's warrior society, warriors wore war paint for spiritual protection. Comanches used black and white; Crows had red-striped faces for horse-stealing raids; and Blackfeet painted a white line across the face for vengeance.

Comanche

Crow

Weapons of war

An elk-horn bow could fire fatal arrows over a short range, but for closer combat a warrior favoured a tomahawk or war club. Lances were thrust forwards to dismount or gut an enemy rider. Most warriors also carried a shield for protection.

shield

tomahawk

war club

quiver holding bow and arrows

war lance

Blackfeet

The warrior society was a kind of club that selected men of the tribe belonged to. In battle the warriors followed the war chief, a man picked for his leadership and fighting skills. In peacetime the warriors acted as the tribe's police force. They were known for their discipline and fierceness. Loyalty to their tribe and their society was to the death.

The Sun Dance ceremony

A warrior committed himself to his tribe by taking part in a religious ceremony called the Sun Dance. For eight days he had no food or drink and gazed straight into the Sun. He wore body paint and his chest was pierced with skewers, tied by thongs to a sacred pole. He danced and jerked until the flesh gave way, leaving scars which he wore with pride.

Religion and myth

To every American Indian, the land and the spirit life were the most important matters in the world. All tribes believed in a spiritual force that was in the earth, animals, the sky and everything around them. They paid their respect in rituals and ceremonies, some adopting elements from Christianity brought by the Spanish.

A young girl's vigil

Every young teenager performed a vigil as part of their journey into adulthood. Catherine Wabose became her tribe's prophetess after her vigil. Following a six-day fast, she heard a supernatural voice tell her to walk along a shining path. First she met 'Everlasting Standing Woman', then 'Little Man Spirit' who said his name would be her first son's name. 'Bright Blue Sky' gave her the gift of life. Finally she received the gift of prophecy.

Sweat it out

Though it varied from tribe to tribe, the sweat lodge ceremony was universal among American Indians. It was used to purify the soul or heal sickness. The sweat lodge was dome-shaped, built with saplings and covered with blankets or hide. It seated about six people. A leader in charge of the ceremony threw herbs and water over the heated stones in a firepit which gave off purifying steam. The participants sat in the lodge chanting and praying to the spirits.

Many dances, prayers and ceremonies were performed for special occasions. An American Indian's life – and death – was spent trying to please the spirits. Tribes such as the Dakota built tall platforms on which they placed their dead, to bring them closer to the sky. So that a tribe's history was not forgotten, mythical stories were handed down by word of mouth from generation to generation.

The Ghost Dance

The Ghost Dance was practised by Indians of the Plains and Great Basin. A Paiute prophet named Wovoka told his ghost dancers that praying, chanting and dancing in circles for days would bring back dead relatives, the buffalo, and even return the land to the way it had been before Europeans came. The ghost dancers wore shirts covered in symbols which were said to protect them from harm.

61

RANCHES & RANCHERS

The Spanish brought over the first cattle. After Texan independence, millions of longhorns were left roaming free. Young men went to make their fortunes by rounding up and claiming the wild herds as their own.

Springtime round-up
In spring, the cattle were driven down from their winter pasture into corrals. Riders would rope the new calves and drag them to the branding crew. The red-hot iron marked the calves with their owner's brand for life.

Line riders
The first ranches had no fences. Their boundaries were natural barriers, such as rivers. Line riders worked the remotest parts of the ranch making sure the cattle stayed on their side of the range, or line.

Food for all

Out in the middle of nowhere, a ranch had to be self-sufficient. Milk came from the dairy cows, eggs from the hen-house, and water from a stream or well. Meat was plentiful and a small kitchen garden supplied fresh vegetables.

Who's in charge?

When a ranch owner was away on business, the foreman was in charge. He hired and fired everyone from the cook, to the cowboys, wranglers and bronc-busters.

There was plenty of free grass and good water in the West – important ingredients for fattening cows. Cowboys drove the cattle to the nearest cow town, and from there the animals were carried east by train. Demand grew and 'cattle barons' grew rich. Charles Goodnight was one of the best-known barons – he's also famous for inventing the chuck wagon so his cowboys could eat well on the trail. John and Elizabeth Iliff supplied beef to the Union Pacific Railroad, buying up to 15,000 steers a year.

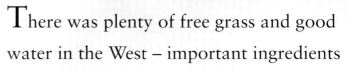

Charles Goodnight

Elizabeth Iliff

Richard King's running W

Mifflin Kenedy's laurel leaf

rocking chair

hog eye

broken arrow

Brands

The best way to know who owned a steer was to read its brand. It was finders keepers if you found an orphaned calf with no brand (known as a maverick). Anyone could claim the unmarked calf and brand it as his own.

scissors

pipe

63

A cowboy and his horse

The first cowboys were American Indians, taught to look after cattle by Spanish missionaries in Mexico. Mexican *vaqueros* came next. Theirs is the language of the cowboy: *lazo* became 'lasso', *reata* 'lariat' and *chaperjos* 'chaps'. Known everywhere as 'cowboys', other names for them include 'cowpuncher', 'cowhand' and 'buckaroo', depending on which part of the country they worked in.

cowgirl
(Montana)

vaquero
(Mexico, S. California, Arizona)

buckaroo
(California, Nevada, Oregon)

cowpuncher
(New Mexico, Texas)

Rough 'n' tough
Unlike the Hollywood image, real-life cowboys were honest, hard-working, and friendly to strangers. The land was harsh and many suffered from rheumatism, eye diseases and damaged spines. Most walked bow-legged from years in the saddle!

hat

Quarter Horse

bridle

gloves

bandanna

revolver

slicker

brand

bit

reins

saddle

lariat

blanket

chaps

spurs

stirrup

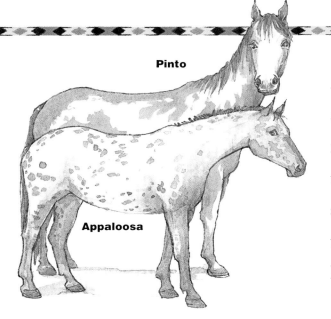

Pinto

Appaloosa

A cowboy chose a horse suited to the job and found a gelding more reliable than a mare. The strong, agile Quarter Horse was the most popular breed with cowboys. But some selected a horse for its looks, such as the Appaloosa, favourite of the Nez Percé Indians, or the dappled Pinto.

Spurs & saddles

Often called 'gentle persuaders', spurs were used to control a horse. Sharp new spurs had the points blunted. There were two main styles of saddle, the Texas (1) and the California (2). A saddle lasted a lifetime and there was an old cowboy saying that 'to sell your saddle' meant you were broke.

fancy spurs

workaday spurs

1

2

Cowboy gear

The cowboy's leather boots were handmade. Five-centimetre high heels prevented the foot slipping out of the stirrup. The cowboy's hat, often a Stetson, had a broad brim to shade the eyes from the sun and a tall crown to keep the head cool. Chaps, made of either leather or wool, were worn over jeans to protect the legs from thorns or prickly cacti. Having water could make the difference between life or death, so the cowboy kept his canteen full and close to hand. A sougan, or quilted blanket, kept him warm at night. The cowboy's rifle was used for hunting and protection. So he wasn't hampered on horseback, the cowboy's rifle and bed roll were carried in the chuck wagon.

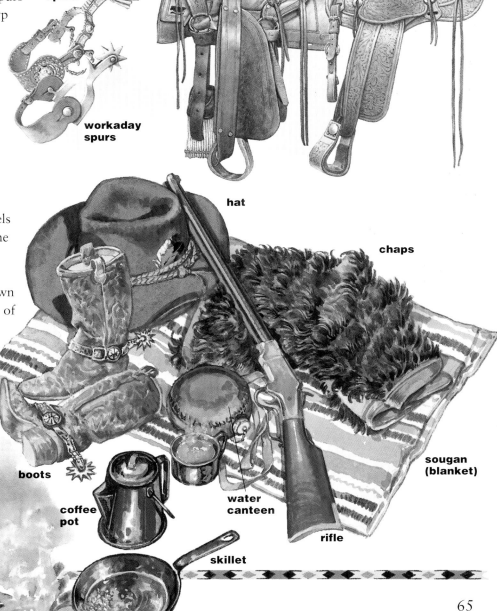

hat

chaps

boots

coffee pot

water canteen

rifle

skillet

sougan (blanket)

On the trail

On a cattle drive, there was one cowboy to every 250 cattle. A 2,000 kilometre long drive took about four months and, on average, the cowboy earnt $30 per month. The trail boss headed the column, which could be as wide as 3 kilometres. At the sides, flank riders stopped the steers wandering away, while at the back the drag riders pushed them forwards.

Life on the trail

Up an hour before dawn, a cowboy spent up to 14 hours in the saddle every day. The men took turns keeping watch at night.

Danger!

River crossings were a hazardous time, as many of the cowboys couldn't swim. It didn't take much to stampede nervous cattle. Thunderstorms, grass fires, even a cowboy sneezing could set them running!

flank riders

chuck wagon

trail boss

Cattle-trail blazers

The cattle routes had to be carved out of the harsh terrain. Rancher Charles Goodnight and his partner Oliver Loving founded the Goodnight-Loving Trail; Joseph McCoy's route used part of the Chisholm Trail; Granville Stuart drove his steers across Oregon to Montana; and Lucien Maxwell cut a new route to Nebraska called the Western Trail.

humped Brahman

Texas longhorn

Hereford

British shorthorn

drag riders

Breeds of cow

'Critters', 'beeves' or 'dogies' were the cowboys' favourite nicknames for cattle. The Texas longhorn was the predominant cow in the Southwest. Later, the shorthorn, the Hereford and the humped Brahman were introduced. They provided better meat and were immune to 'Texas fever'.

Campfire songs

A sweet-singing cowboy entertained the men and calmed the cattle. There were rousing trail-driving songs, like *The Old Chisholm Trail*, as well as gentle lullabies.

The Night Herding Song

Oh say, little dogies, when you goin' to lay down, and give up this driftin' and rovin' around?

My horse is leg-weary and I'm awful tired, but if you get away, I'm sure to be fired.

Lay down, little dogies, lay down, hi-o, hi-o, hi-o.

▲ The chuck wagon and campfire were a focal point on the drive. Bacon, bread and beans were usually on the menu, but dried and canned food helped vary the meals. Strong black coffee was a must with every meal.

Cow towns

 After long months on the trail, the cowboy hit town. After a quick bath and shave, he threw away his old, torn jeans and put on his new 'store-boughts'. Then he headed for the nearest saloon. His favourite drinks were whiskey and beer. On a drunken spree, the cowboy often terrorized the ordinary town citizens. Forget the fist fights in the movies – 'manstoppers' (guns) and knives were the norm. More often than not, a cowboy headed back to camp with an empty wallet and a sore head!

Hitting the saloon

Whether it was a tent, a Mexican *cantina* or a saloon, the bar was a place where men could relax, have a drink and a meal, play cards or listen to music. Lonesome cowboys could pay a dollar to dance with a girl. Many saloons became famous, such as The Bucket of Blood Saloon, The Jersey Lilly and The Occidental.

In the bar

The bar took up a lot of space and was well-stocked with bottled wines, whiskey and other spirits. There was home-brewed beer, as well as imported ale from England and stout from Ireland. The saloon also sold home-baked food and luxuries such as pickled eggs or cheese.

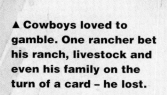

▲ Cowboys loved to gamble. One rancher bet his ranch, livestock and even his family on the turn of a card – he lost.

Horsin' around

Cowboys were noted for bad behaviour when they hit town. After months of hard work, they let off steam. The sheriff would lock up a drunken cowboy causing trouble, and not let him out till he was sober.

▲ *In Without Knocking*, by Charles Russell

While stock buyers and cattlemen frequented fancy hotel bars, cowboys went to the cheaper saloons. Hispanic and black cowboys were often forced to drink in separate saloons. Cow towns attracted all sorts: gunmen, outlaws, thieves and gamblers. The Kansas cow town of Abilene employed respected lawmen, such as Wild Bill Hickok and Bat Masterson, to keep the peace.

▼ The cow town was the place where the trail met the railroad. Towns like Wichita, Ellsworth and Abilene flourished because of the cattle business. Stock buyers came from the East to buy whole herds to load on trains for New York and Chicago.

◄ To increase profits, bar owners used to employ female singers. They were accompanied by a pianist, violinist or banjo player. Some put on a whole night of theatrical acts with jugglers and knife throwers.

WESTWARD HO!

Between 1836 and 1890 nearly 750,000 people crossed the western frontier. They came from all over the world, lured by the promise of land and a better future. The Mormons headed west to escape persecution and find their own 'promised land'. They settled near the Great Salt Lake in Utah in June 1847. And, when gold was discovered in California in 1848, it sparked a rush of fortune-seekers.

The trip from Independence to Oregon City covered 3,700 km and took six months. Pioneers said: "The weak died on the way and courage never left."

There wasn't room on the wagon for everyone and many made the long journey on foot. Wagons often broke down and heavy furniture was discarded along the way to lighten the load.

Westward trails

With no highways to get from place to place, American Indians and Spanish adventurers had to find their own way. Later, explorers and traders followed the same routes. Settlers' wagons widened them into dusty trails. These formed a vast network across the prairies, deserts and mountains of the West.

Heading into unknown land had its dangers. Death by drowning, cholera, smallpox or accidental shootings was all too common. Many babies and young children didn't finish the trip. Livestock died from exhaustion or from eating poisonous plants. Hostile American Indians would often steal cattle, oxen and horses.

Stocking a Conestoga wagon didn't come cheap. Buying enough farm tools, furniture, food and clothing for a family of up to 16 could cost an incredible $1,500 – almost five years' wages!

Staking a claim

At their journey's end, pioneers claimed their land by putting up a marker. The Homestead Act of 1862 allowed a settler 65 hectares of land for just $10 – so long as he stayed and improved the land for at least five years.

Making a home

Early pioneers built their homes with whatever nature provided. Log cabins were built in the forests of the Northwest. On the plains there were few trees, so cave-like homes were dug into the sides of hills. These tended to collapse, so sod houses took their place. When they could afford to, settlers replaced these with more permanent structures.

A soddy

It took 4,000 square metres of turf to cut enough bricks to build a sod house or 'soddy'. The owners were nicknamed sodbusters.

Doors and windows

Doors were made from packing cases. Greased paper kept out the wind until the settlers could afford glass windows.

Soddy life

Nature played havoc with sodbusters. Droughts were common. In a summer storm, bolts of lightning might set the prairies on fire. There were destructive twisters and dust storms. Plagues of locusts ate all the crops. In winter, blizzards froze the earth and the people.

Keeping warm

On the treeless plains there were no logs to use as fuel for cooking and heating. Sunflowers and greasewood were burned instead, but more often buffalo or cow dung, known as 'chips', was gathered. It made the house smelly but at least everyone was warm!

It was hard work growing up in a pioneer family. Young children had to milk the cows, feed the chickens and tend the horses. The lucky ones attended school, with children of all ages in the one class – but they still had to do their chores. Illness and disease struck many families. Cholera and smallpox were killers. The nearest doctor might live many kilometres away, so the pioneers treated themselves with home-made remedies.

Water for life

Homesteaders couldn't survive without water. Some relied on a nearby river or creek, or collected rainwater in barrels. Others dug wells or used windmills to pump water up out of the ground.

▲ Though work was shared around, women did the cooking, cleaning, and washing as well as helping with the crops and animals.

A lighter side to life

A visit to the general store was a family outing. The nearest shop could be up to 150 kilometres away, in the middle of nowhere, or in a town. Visiting the store was a chance to meet people as well as stock up on provisions.

The general store

A typical general store stocked everything you could think of: dry goods, groceries, tinned food, sweets, bolts of cloth, shoes, clothes, lanterns, weapons and farm tools. The shopkeeper provided chairs and a fire to make his customers feel welcome. People spent hours here catching up on news and gossip.

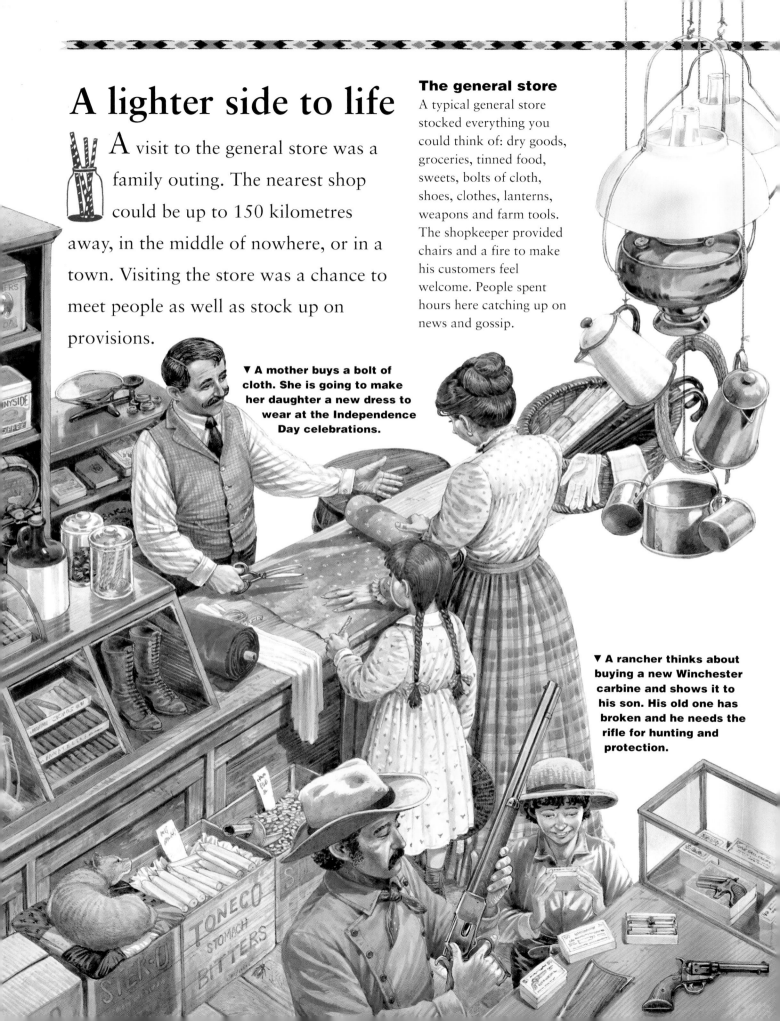

▼ A mother buys a bolt of cloth. She is going to make her daughter a new dress to wear at the Independence Day celebrations.

▼ A rancher thinks about buying a new Winchester carbine and shows it to his son. His old one has broken and he needs the rifle for hunting and protection.

The wish book

Mail-order catalogues stocked everything from everyday items to luxuries. There was even a catalogue for the lonesome man who wished to order a bride!

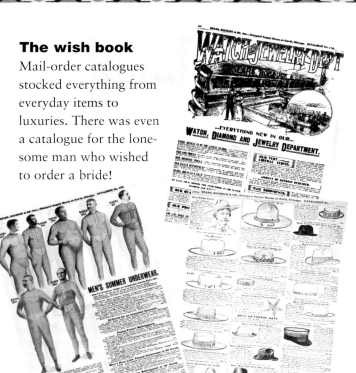

The quilting bee

Neighbouring homesteads were far apart. Women took a break from their chores and gathered at one another's homes to swap gossip and make quilts. These 'bees' lasted days – it could be ages before they got together again.

Fun at the fair

There were many ways that teenage boys could show off their strength and skills at the county fair. Pig-wrestling was dirty and fun. Other contests were frog-jumping, foot races, games of catch and even baseball.

What little spare time settlers had, they liked to spend enjoying themselves. Every town in America held a parade to celebrate Independence Day. A wedding, a new house, or a barn-raising was a big event. So were dances, horse races, boxing matches and county fairs. There was plenty of food and drink, and a chance for people to meet old friends and make new ones.

Mine
In search of the rich veins of gold, miners used pickaxes and dynamite to dig cave-like mines in the mountain-side. The rubble was then shovelled into the sluice.

Sluice
As the rubble from the mine passed down the long sluice, or trough, water washed away the lighter debris to leave behind the heavier gold buried inside the rock.

Cash office
Inside the cash or assays office, gold dust and nuggets were weighed and traded for ready cash.

Laundry
Many Chinese were discriminated against in the gold mines. They found a way to make money out of the Gold Rush by opening camp laundries.

Gold rush!

"Gold! Gold on the American River!" With these words, Sam Brannan started the 1849 rush of fortune-seekers to California. Some came overland along the Oregon Trail; others sailed to San Francisco. Known as the forty-niners, the prospectors included more than 17,000 Chinese immigrants. Mining camps, or diggings, sprang up with names like Sixbit Gulch, Whiskey Flat and Hangtown.

California wasn't the only place with gold. The Black Hills of Dakota were sacred lands for the northern Plains tribes, and lands that the government had promised them they could keep. But after the 7th Cavalry found gold in the region, thousands of gold-seekers headed for the hills.

Fortunes
A miner working his own diggings could make lots of money. Twenty-five grams of gold was worth $16. Working seven days a week, a miner could find enough gold to earn himself almost $2,000.

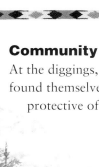

Community

At the diggings, miners of the same nationality soon found themselves living close together. They were very protective of their mines and looked after one another.

Muleback tuck shop

Miners didn't have time to waste cooking luxuries like bread. So they were willing to part with a dollar a loaf when the baker came by with freshly-baked bread. Women soon found they could make money by charging for meals. Some went on to be successful hotel owners.

▲ As fast as they sprang up, the mining towns also disappeared. Once every last bit of gold had been mined, there was nothing to keep people there. They packed their bags and headed for the next diggings, leaving a 'ghost town' behind them.

Panning for gold

There were several ways to get gold out of the creek. One man would put rubble from the river-bed into a 'rocker' as another man moved it back and forth in the flow of water – any gold was caught in a sieve below. Panning was another cheap and easy method. A handful of gravel or sand was put into a pan, then swirled around with water to wash away the lighter sand, leaving the heavy gold behind.

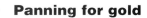

THE MAIN SITES OF TOMBSTONE

1 St Paul's Episcopal Church (under construction)
2 Mexican quarter
3 Hop Town – the Chinese quarter
4 new Cochise County Courthouse (under construction)
5 C.S. Fly's photographic studio
6 newspaper office: *Tombstone Epitaph*
7 City Hall (under construction)
8 original Courthouse
9 newspaper office: *Tombstone Nugget*
10 Schieffelin Hall (theatre)
11 post office
12 Jack Crabtree's Lexington livery stable
13 Catholic church (under construction)
14 women's boarding houses
15 Wells Fargo office
16 ice-cream parlour
17 OK Corral
18 US customs office
19 Occidental Saloon
20 Watt & Tarbell's undertaking parlour
21 The Crystal Palace Saloon (US Deputy Marshal's office above)
22 The Oriental Saloon
23 city bakery
24 The Birdcage Theater
25 Western Union telegraph office
26 courtroom
27 first public school (temporary)
28 Wing Woo Lung laundry
29 miners' cabins
30 fire station

Why 'Tombstone'?
When Ed Schieffelin's party began prospecting in Arizona, someone said all they were likely to find would be tombstones. Instead they struck silver, but they named the new settlement 'Tombstone'!

A frontier town

Not all towns in the West depended on the cattle trade for their existence. The discovery of rich mineral deposits could herald the coming of a frontier town. Tombstone, Arizona began this way when silver was discovered there by prospector Ed Schieffelin in 1877.

Between 1877 and 1880, the populaton of Tombstone grew to 10,000. The town was a centre for businesses, fortune-seekers, gamblers and outlaws.

IXTH STREET

30

Town folk

There were many people in town who depended on the success of Tombstone's mines for their livelihood. The miners came from different cultures and businesses sprang up to cater for everyone's needs. There were newspapers, saloons, hotels, schools and churches.

JOBS IN TOMBSTONE
1 newspaper editor
2 undertaker
3 blacksmith
4 travelling preacher
5 actress
6 school teacher
7 mayor

Allen Street

Allen Street was one of Tombstone's main roads. It was lined with shops, hotels, banks and saloons.

The street was nearly 25 metres wide. It had raised wooden sidewalks instead of paving stones, and no street lights.

Tombstone is the site of the most famous gunfight in the West. Yet the gunfight at the OK Corral lasted only 30 seconds. Wyatt Earp, his brothers Morgan and Virgil, and Doc Holliday fought Ike and Billy Clanton, and Tom and Frank McLaury to end a long feud. The McLaurys and Billy Clanton were killed; Morgan and Virgil Earp and Doc Holliday were wounded.

DEADLY DAYS

Outlaws were a threat to the frontier way of life. Some people stole rather than worked for a living. There were stage-coach robbers, cattle rustlers, land barons (who stole other people's claims), gamblers and train robbers – to name but a few.

Stage-coaches

Before the railroad was built, the stage was the main form of transport for passengers and mail. There were many types of stage-coach, but none more famous than the Wells Fargo *Concorde*.

The loot

Passenger stage-coaches often carried money. The strongbox held company payrolls in coins or gold, and this was the robbers' main target. Of course, they robbed the passengers as well!

The gang

Outlaws operated alone or in gangs. The Hole in the Wall Gang – if records are to be believed – had over one hundred members from different gangs, including the Wild Bunch led by Butch Cassidy.

The one thing that an outlaw's life depended on was his weapon. Early revolvers had paper cartridges with lead bullets and were classed as cap and ball pistols. These were later replaced with brass-jacketed bullets of different calibres (or sizes). The revolver was used for fighting at close quarters, the rifle or carbine for long-distance shooting. The threat of a shotgun was enough to scare anyone, and many outlaws sawed down the barrel to make the weapon easier to carry.

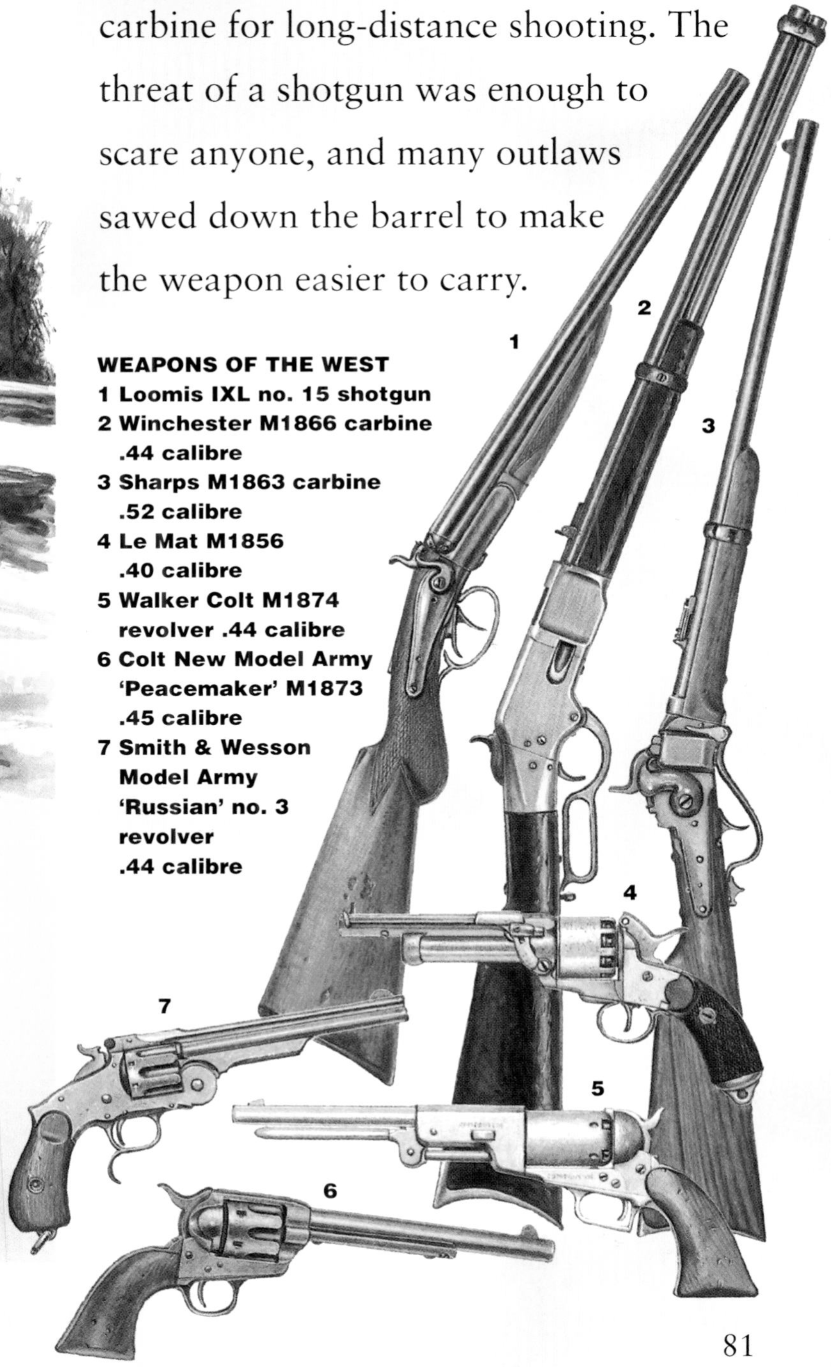

WEAPONS OF THE WEST
1 Loomis IXL no. 15 shotgun
2 Winchester M1866 carbine
   .44 calibre
3 Sharps M1863 carbine
   .52 calibre
4 Le Mat M1856
   .40 calibre
5 Walker Colt M1874
   revolver .44 calibre
6 Colt New Model Army
   'Peacemaker' M1873
   .45 calibre
7 Smith & Wesson
   Model Army
   'Russian' no. 3
   revolver
   .44 calibre

(1867–c. 1910)
Once a cavalry scout, the Apache Kid killed a man, escaped and went on to become a ruthless killer and robber who menaced New Mexico and Arizona.

(1848–1889)
Belle Starr was the leader of a gang of horse and cattle rustlers. She and her Cherokee husband, Sam, had a $1,000 reward on their heads.

(1853–1895)
Hardin was one of the most feared gunmen in Texas. After killing a black slave, he ambushed and killed the three Union soldiers sent to arrest him.

(1876–unknown)
Cattle Annie once rode with the Doolin Gang. She and her partner, Little Britches, were famous cattle rustlers, known as 'Oklahoma's girl bandits'.

Billy the Kid (1859–1881)
He was only 22 years old when he died, but William H. Bonney, or Billy the Kid, left his mark. He killed his first man when he was 12 years old and was involved in a ranch war known as the Lincoln County War. After 'the Kid' killed two deputies in New Mexico, Sheriff Pat Garrett hunted him down and shot him.

Outlaws and gunslingers

The best-known outlaws were the man-killers. Bloody Bill Anderson, Rufus Buck, Joaquin Murieta and John Brown were all cold-blooded murderers. After fighting in the Civil War, some, such as Frank and Jesse James, couldn't fit back into normal civilian life. They took to robbery with a large gang of other ex-soldiers. Lone bandit Black Bart eluded the law for eight years, robbing Wells Fargo stages. He had come to California to seek his fortune, and had tried his hand at panning for gold before taking up his life of crime.

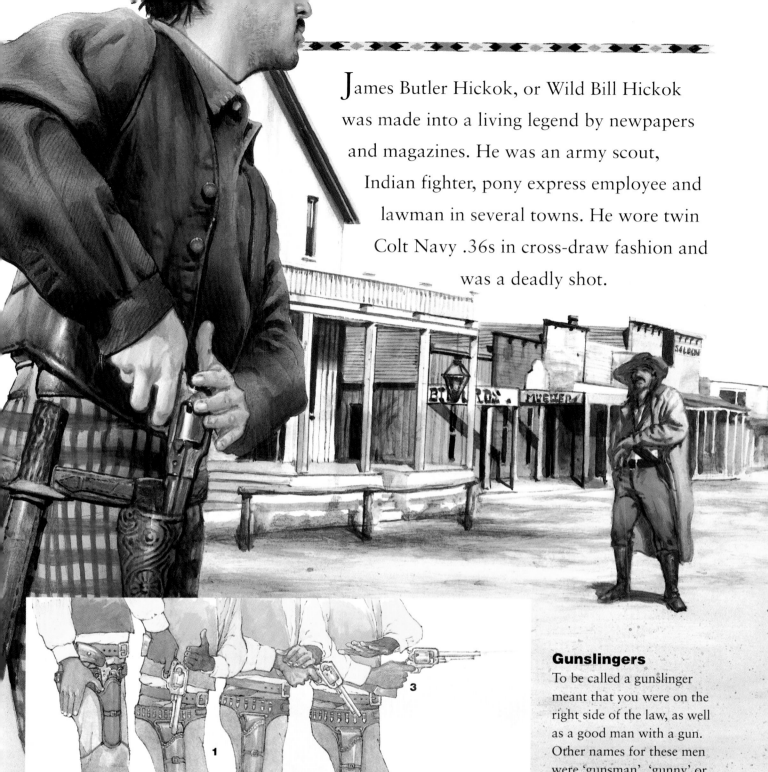

James Butler Hickok, or Wild Bill Hickok was made into a living legend by newpapers and magazines. He was an army scout, Indian fighter, pony express employee and lawman in several towns. He wore twin Colt Navy .36s in cross-draw fashion and was a deadly shot.

Fast on the draw

'Fanning' a revolver is the fastest way to fire more than one bullet. Gripping the butt of the pistol in one hand, with the index finger holding back the trigger (1), the palm of the other hand hauls back (or fans) the hammer (2) once for each bullet to be fired. As the pistol comes up level, the hammer is fully cocked and springs forward in one go (3).

Gunslingers

To be called a gunslinger meant that you were on the right side of the law, as well as a good man with a gun. Other names for these men were 'gunsman', 'gunny' or 'gun shark'. Whether he wore one pistol or two, a gunslinger's weapons were always on display to show he meant business – he would always use his pistols first and ask questions later.

83

Law and order

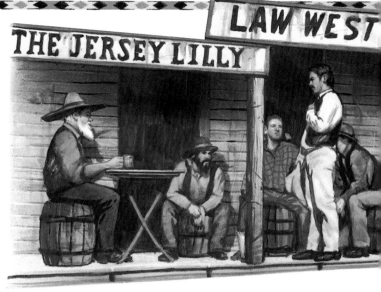

Coping with criminals on the frontier was a problem. The vastness of the area was too much for the official police force. In some places ordinary men became vigilantes and fought the outlaws themselves. The Cattle Ranchers Association hired range detectives to catch rustlers. Gunslingers were hired to guard banks, railroads and mines. The most famous peace-officer was the marshal. Towns hired marshals and deputies to enforce their laws.

Law west of the Pecos

Roy Bean was nearly 60 years old when he came to the little town of Langtry, Texas and became Justice of the Peace. Self-taught in law, he set up a courtroom in his saloon where he was judge for almost 20 years. He was in love with the English actress Lily Langtry and named his saloon the Jersey Lilly after her. Known for his strange rulings, he once fined a dead man $40 for illegally carrying a weapon!

Badge of office

Law officers wore badges to show what job they held. There were many designs, just as there were different jobs. A US marshal was responsible for the whole state. The town marshal and deputies looked after the town for the government. The protection of local people, homes and businesses was down to the sheriff and his deputies. The famed Texas Rangers were formed by Stephen F. Austin in 1823 to help enforce the law and they still operate today.

Pinkerton

Civil War veteran Allen Pinkerton's Detective Agency made a business out of capturing wanted men. The agency fought against the James Gang and the Wild Bunch. It was the first to keep files, with details of solved and unsolved crimes and photographs of criminals, like the files used by the FBI today.

When criminals were caught they had to be punished, just like today. For lesser crimes, such as being drunk and disorderly, or carrying a weapon in public, there was just a fine. Not all towns had jails – one prisoner was kept overnight under a tarpaulin staked to the ground! More serious crimes were punishable by death. Some states issued an 'invite to a necktie party', where the public could witness a hanging.

Own justice
Luke Short formed the Dodge City Peace Commission after being kicked out of town by the mayor, because of the goings-on in his saloon. The Commission, which included fellow-gunmen Bill Tilghman, Bat Masterson, Wyatt Earp and Doc Holliday among others, escorted Short back into town. With such strong backing, Short was allowed to run his saloon just as he pleased!

Characters of the West

Thomas Hart Benton
(1782–1858)
As a politician representing Mississippi, championed the cause for America's 'Manifest Destiny' – the right of the US to expand its land westward.

John Butterfield
(1801–1869)
Operated the Butterfield Overland Mail Service between Missouri and San Francisco from 1858 to 1861. He sold the firm to Wells Fargo and went on to develop a new venture – American Express.

Martha Jane Canary (Calamity Jane)
(c. 1848–1903)
Many stories abound about Jane but she definitely loved Wild Bill Hickok and is buried next to him in Deadwood, Dakota. She was a good shot, often dressed as a man and drove wagon teams for the Union Pacific Railroad.

Christopher (Kit) Carson
(1809–1868)
Famed as a fur trapper, explorer, scout and Indian fighter. Carson spoke French, Spanish and Indian languages.

Cochise (c. 1815–1874)
Renegade chief of the Chiricahua Apaches. He led his warriors on raids on settlers and miners throughout Arizona and even into Mexico.

William F. Cody (Buffalo Bill) (1846–1917)
The dime novelist Ned Buntline wrote of Buffalo Bill's exploits in 1869. Cody rode the pony express and was an army scout. In 1883 he began his famous Wild West Show.

Samuel Colt (1814–1862)
Designed a new, more reliable six-shooter by adapting the old five-shot revolver. His .45 'Peacemaker' was one of the most widely-used guns in the West.

Crazy Horse (Tashunka Witco) (c. 1841–1877)
One of the most aggressive Dakota chiefs who fought at Rosebud and Little Big Horn.

George Crook (1828–1890)
Army general who campaigned against the Apache and Dakota. He tried to get better treatment for Geronimo and other Apaches after their surrender.

Isom Dart
(c. 1849–1900)
Born a slave, he fought with the Confederates. He became a cattle rustler and bronc-buster. He ended his days a rancher.

John Deere (1804–1886)
Inventor of the self-polishing steel plough, used by the settlers on the plains. In 1836, he founded Deere & Co, a farm machinery company that still operates today.

Wyatt Berry Stapp Earp
(1848–1929)
Lawman in Wichita, Dodge City and Tombstone. He owned gambling halls and saloons from the 1870s, but is best known for his involvement in the gunfight at the OK Corral.

Alice Fletcher (1838–1923)
A white woman who lived among American Indian tribes in Nebraska. In 1883, she became an Indian agent and helped survey the land to be shared among the tribes. The American Indians called her 'Measuring Woman'.

Captain John Charles Frémont (1818–1890)
Early explorer of the West, nicknamed 'Great Pathfinder'. Kit Carson was his guide. His wife's account of his journeys was a bestseller.

Pat F. Garrett (1850–1908)
Former buffalo hunter and cowboy, he was sheriff of Lincoln County when he killed Billy the Kid. He later became a rancher and was shot dead in a feud.

Geronimo (Goyathly)
(1829–1909)
Chiricahua Apache who led his people against both Mexicans and Americans. He finally surrendered and lived on a Florida reservation from 1887.

Charles Goodnight
(1836–1929)
One of the great cattle barons. After success with Oliver Loving, he teamed up with fellow rancher John Adair in 1877. By 1888 he was worth $500,000.

Sam Houston (1793–1863)
He led the Texans at San Jacinto in the military drive to gain Texan independence from Mexico. In 1836 he was sworn in as the first president of the Republic of Texas.

Chief Joseph
(1832–1904)
Not wanting to fight over land, Chief Joseph moved his tribe, the Nez Percés. The army pursued them, starting a three-month battle. The chief surrendered and he and his tribe were put on a reservation.

Oliver Loving (1813–1867)
Trailed herds to Colorado and Illinois before the Civil War. In 1866, he teamed up with Charles Goodnight to combine herds and cowboys.

Susan Shelby Magoffin
(1827–1855)
The first white woman to travel the Santa Fe Trail. She wrote a diary which was published in 1926.

James W. Marshall
(1810–1885)
Carpenter working on the American River, whose discovery of gold led to the California Gold Rush of 1849.

William Barclay (Bat) Masterson (1853–1921)
Railroader, buffalo hunter, saloon owner and gambler who found fame as a lawman. He was elected sheriff of Ford County in 1877 and was later a Dodge City marshal.

Marie Gilbert (Lola) Montez (1818–1861)
Originally from Ireland, Lola was an actress of dazzling beauty who entertained the miners across the California gold region.

Annie Oakley (1860–1926)
Found fame in Buffalo Bill's Wild West Show as 'Little Miss Sure-Shot'. She could outshoot her husband, Frank Butler, a well-known exhibition shooter.

Isaac Parker (1838–1896)
An Arizona judge, whose handling of outlaws soon got him the nickname of the 'Hanging Judge'. He even built a set of gallows that could hang more than one person at a time.

Red Cloud (1822–1909)
Dakota chief who successfully defended his land and closed many settlers' routes. He became leader of the Indians on reservations, and after the signing of the Fort Laramie Treaty he forced the US government to keep its terms.

Sacajawea (1778– *either* 1812 *or* 1884)
The Shoshoni wife of French-Canadian fur trapper Toussant Charbonneau who acted as a guide and interpreter for the Corps of Discovery.

William Tecumseh Sherman (1820–1891)
A Union general famed for his Civil War exploits. After the war, he took control of building forts across the West. He was in charge of the entire US army between 1869 and 1884, leading aggressive campaigns against the American Indians.

John B. Stetson (1830–1906)
Hatmaker from Philadelphia whose famous hat, the Stetson, is sometimes also called Boss of the Plains, a John B or a JB.

William Matthew Tilghman (1854–1924)
Renowned as a buffalo hunter and crack shot, he served as Dodge City's first marshal. He moved to Oklahoma, where he was one of the 'Three Guardsmen' (along with Chris Madsen and Heck Thomas), who hunted down the Doolin and Dalton Gangs.

Sarah Winnemucca
(1844–1891)
Paiute who negotiated for better conditions for her tribe. In 1883 she wrote an autobiography, *Life Among the Paiutes*, telling the plight of her tribe.

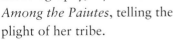

Brigham Young (1801–1877)
Religious leader who led the Mormons from Nauvoo, Illinois, where they were being persecuted for their beliefs, to Utah to settle on the shores of the Great Salt Lake.

Glossary

To find out the names for parts of a ship and sails, turn to pages 22-25.

anchor Heavy metal hooked object on a long chain, thrown into the water to stop a boat from moving.

archaeologist Someone who studies historical remains of things people have made or built, such as ruins and shipwrecks.

assays office Where miners had their gold weighed and priced.

backstaff An instrument once used to measure a ship's position.

ballast Any heavy material used to weigh down a ship, to make it stable.

barnacles Small creatures that encrust underwater rocks and ships' timbers.

barracks Soldiers' sleeping quarters.

bend Knot used by sailors to tie two pieces of rope together.

bilge-water Foul water that collected in the bottom of old sailing ships.

blackjack

blackjack Any of the black-and-white pirate flags used from the 1690s onwards.

block and tackle Pulley and ropes.

blockade To prevent shipping or supplies reaching a port.

booty Goods that are stolen or won by violence, especially in times of war.

bosun (or boatswain) The foreman of a crew who looks after the ship's masts, sails and flags.

bowline knot Knot which makes a loop at the end of a rope.

bowsprit A long spar sticking out from the bow, at the front of a sailing ship.

brand The mark burned into the hide of a cow or horse to show who owned it.

branding Using a brand to show who owns a cow or horse.

bronc-buster Someone who tamed wild, 'unbroken' horses for cowboys to ride.

bronco A wild horse, a mustang.

buccaneer One of the outlaws who settled on Caribbean islands from the 1630s onwards and took up piracy.

buffalo Shaggy wild cattle, also known as American bison.

buffalo chip Dried buffalo dung used as fuel on the plains.

calibre The diameter of a bullet, measured in hundredths of an inch.

cannibalism Eating other people.

cannon A large gun mounted on wheels.

cap and ball Early revolver loaded at the front of the cylinder.

capstan A winding machine pushed around by the crew of a sailing vessel to raise the anchor.

caravel A small three-masted sailing ship used by the Spanish and Portuguese in the 1400s and early 1500s.

capstan

carbine A short, light rifle.

careening Beaching a ship for cleaning and repairs.

cartridge A small case holding a gun's gunpowder or bullets.

castle A high fighting deck on either end of a medieval warship. The term 'forecastle' (front deck) survived as fo'c'sle.

cattle baron Owner of a vast cattle empire. Also known as a cattle king.

cattle drive Herding a group of cattle along a trail to be sold.

caulking Making a wooden ship waterproof with oakum and tar.

chaps Tough leggings worn over a cowboy's trousers to protect the legs.

chart A map of oceans and coastlines.

chuck wagon A mobile cook-house used on round-ups and cattle drives. The chuck box at the back stored food, utensils and medicine.

Civil War War between the northern and southern states of the US, 1861–1865.

claim To have the legal right over the ownership of a mine, farm or grazing land.

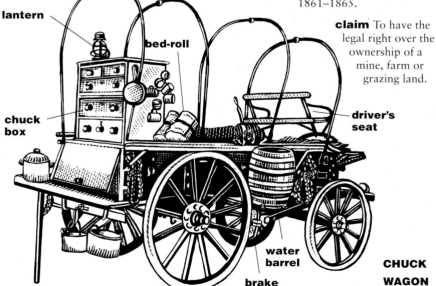

lantern

bed-roll

chuck box

driver's seat

water barrel

brake

CHUCK WAGON

colony (1) An overseas settlement. (2) A country ruled by another country.

commission Authorization for a privateer to attack enemy shipping.

compass A magnetic navigational instrument used to find north.

compensation Money paid to make up for an injury or loss.

compass

Conestoga wagon A boat-shaped load-carrying wagon used by the pioneers. It was usually pulled along by oxen.

conquistator A Spanish soldier who came to America in the 1500s in search of gold.

corral Fenced enclosure for cattle or horses.

corsair (1) A pirate or privateer, especially from the Mediterranean Sea or northern France. (2) The ship used by a corsair.

coup stick A long, lance-like stick with a curved end used by American Indian warriors to touch their enemy but not kill.

cow town A town which sprang up on a cattle trail. Also known as a trail town or cattle town.

cross-draw Style of drawing a revolver where the holster is worn on the hip with the butt of the revolver facing forward. The hand crosses in front of the body to draw the revolver.

cutlass A curved type of naval sword said to have been developed from the hunting-knives of the first buccaneers.

dhow An Arab sailing ship with triangular sails.

dogie (1) An orphan calf. (2) Rancher's nickname for cattle.

figurehead

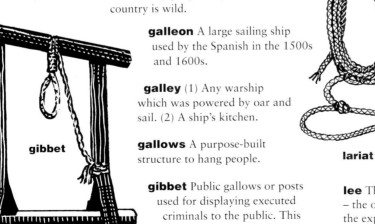

gibbet

doubloon A Spanish gold coin that is no longer used as currency.

dugout canoe A canoe hollowed out from a tree-trunk.

empire A large group of territories ruled by a single government.

evidence Facts put before a court of law during a trial.

fanning A method of shooting a revolver quickly by pulling back the hammer and trigger at the same time.

figurehead A carved and painted wooden figure at the front of a ship.

filibuster (or flibustier) A French buccaneer in the Caribbean.

first mate The second-in-command of a merchant or pirate ship.

fisherman's bend Knot used to tie two ropes of equal thickness together. Often used to attach a rope to an anchor.

fore and aft At the front and at the back of a ship.

fort A building raised for defence, protected by guns.

freebooter Any pirate, privateer or raider.

frontier The furthest edge of land which is settled by people, beyond which the country is wild.

galleon A large sailing ship used by the Spanish in the 1500s and 1600s.

galley (1) Any warship which was powered by oar and sail. (2) A ship's kitchen.

gallows A purpose-built structure to hang people.

gibbet Public gallows or posts used for displaying executed criminals to the public. This practice was meant to deter people from committing similar crimes in the future.

grappling iron

'go on the account' To become a pirate. Slang phrase.

grappling iron Metal hooks used to gain hold of an enemy ship and board it.

Great Father Name for the president of the United States used by American Indians.

grenade A small bomb thrown by hand.

gunslinger Someone skilled with a gun.

hard tack Stale ship's biscuit.

haven A safe harbour or anchorage for ships and boats.

headdress A covering for the head. Headdresses worn by American Indians showed the wearer's position in the tribe.

hitch Knot used to tie a rope to a spar, ring or post.

headdress

hoard A pile of hidden treasure.

holster A pouch to hold a revolver.

hull The outer shell of a ship.

Jolly Roger Any flag flown by a pirate ship to show that its crew should be feared.

junk A large wooden sailing ship used by the Chinese.

keel A single timber running along the bottom of a wooden ship's hull.

knot (1) A method of tying one or more ropes. (2) Speed – one nautical mile per hour (1.852 km/h).

land baron A man who seized land, sometimes dishonestly.

lariat A rope used for catching animals. Known around the West Coast as a lasso.

lariat

lee The sheltered side of a ship or shore – the opposite of 'windward' or 'weather', the exposed side.

letters of marque Official papers of authorization, issued to privateers.

line rider A cowboy who rode to the farthest limit (the line) of a ranch, to stop cows from straying.

logbook The daily record of a ship's voyage and life on board.

longship A ship used by Viking sea-farers.

loot Stolen goods.

lynch To punish someone without a proper trial, usually by hanging.

magazine A gunpowder store.

marlin-spike

marlin-spike A pointed metal tool used for working on ropes.

marlin-spike hitch Knot used to tie a rope or hold a marlin-spike in place.

marooned Left behind on an island, as punishment.

marshal A town's law-enforcer. Also called a policeman.

maverick A stray calf without a brand.

merchant ship A trading ship, carrying goods for sale.

Mormons Members of the Church of Jesus Christ of Latter-Day Saints, established in 1830.

musket A long-barrelled hand gun, an early rifle.

musket

New World A European term for the newly-discovered Americas.

oakum Rope fibres used in caulking.

panning Washing gravel in a pan so only the gold or silver is left behind.

peacepipe A sacred American Indian object that invoked spiritual power when smoked. Also called a medicine pipe.

pemmican American Indian preserved food made of meat, berries and fat.

pieces-of-eight Type of Spanish coinage that are no longer used.

piragua A war canoe used by the buccaneers in the Caribbean.

pirate Someone who attacks shipping or coastal settlements illegally.

Pirate Round A voyage from North America or the Caribbean to West Africa and the Indian Ocean, and back again.

plantation A large estate producing crops such as tobacco, sugar cane or cotton.

plunder Items that have been stolen or seized by force.

pony express A mail service between Missouri and California in 1860 and 1861. Riders covered the 3,164 kilometre trail in less than ten days.

powder horn A container that is used to hold the gunpowder for a musket.

prairie Open grassland.

privateer (1) A person given legal authority to raid enemy merchant shipping and to share the booty. (2) The ship used by a privateer.

prize An enemy ship captured in battle.

ranch A cattle farm. The term includes all the land, buildings and animals owned by the rancher.

remuda A herd of spare horses for cowboys to use.

Rendezvous The month-long meeting between trappers and American Indians held every summer.

REVOLVER

barrel · hammer · chamber · butt · trigger

reservation Land put aside by the government for the use of one or more American Indian tribe.

revolver A handgun. Its chamber revolved to shoot six bullets. Also known as a six-shooter or pistol.

rig The masts and sails of a ship.

rigging The system of ropes used to support the masts and sails of a ship.

rocker A box used by gold miners. Gravel and water were rocked back and forth to sift out the dirt leaving the gold behind.

rodeo A contest or show of cowboy skills.

round-up The gathering together of cattle, for branding, by cowboys.

powder horn

rover A seafarer, often a pirate or rogue.

rudder A hinged board at the back of a ship, for steering.

rum A strong alcoholic drink made from sugar cane.

rustler A cattle or horse thief.

sailcloth Tough canvas used for sails.

scalp A piece of scalp torn off as a sign of victory. Introduced by the Spanish, scalping was adopted by some American Indian tribes.

schooner A fast two-masted sailing ship.

scout A guide or look-out.

scurvy A disease of the skin and gums caused by lack of vitamin C. Sailors often suffered from it because they did not eat enough fruit and vegetables.

scuttling Sinking a ship in one's possession on purpose.

seam The gap between two planks on a wooden ship.

settler Someone who makes a home in a place that is being populated for the first time. Also known as a pioneer.

sheet bend Knot used to tie two ropes of unequal thickness together.

short splice When a piece of rope is lengthened by another of the same size.

skillet A metal frying pan.

slave Someone deprived of their freedom in order to work for someone else.

slicker A waterproof coat.

sloop A swift single-masted sailing vessel.

smuggler Someone who imports goods illegally, to avoid paying tax on them.

soddy A dwelling made of sod turf built by settlers.

sougan A closely-woven or quilted blanket used by a cowboy or cowgirl.

Spanish Main (1) Those parts of the American mainland that were conquered by the Spanish. (2) The whole Caribbean.

spar Any wooden pole used for supporting sails.

Spice Islands An old-fashioned name for the islands of Southeast Asia, where spices are grown.

spices

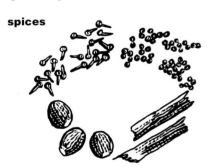

splicing Joining together two ropes.

stage-coach A horse-drawn coach that carries passengers and mail.

steer A male cow that is raised for beef.

Stetson A broad-brimmed, high-crowned felt hat, named after its maker John B. Stetson. Also called Boss of the Plains, a John B.

stickball A ball game for two teams, on which lacrosse is based.

sutler A trader at an army post.

tavern An inn or public house where alcoholic drinks are sold and drunk.

stetson

tax Money paid to the government.

telegraph A way of sending Morse code messages electronically along a wire.

Texas fever An illness in Texas longhorn cattle passed on by ticks.

Texas longhorn Breed of cattle with long horns.

tomahawk An American Indian war-axe used in close combat.

treasure

totem American Indian name for an animal, such as an eagle, or inanimate thing, such as a river, considered to be a spiritual ancestor.

trapper Someone who made their living catching beaver and other wild animals for their fur.

treasure Goods of great value, such as gold and silver.

tribe A community of American Indians who speak the same language and are bound together by ties of blood.

trireme A galley with three banks of oars, used by the Greeks and Romans.

typhoon A violent wind-storm in the Pacific Ocean.

vaquero The name for a cowboy from the Southwest.

vigil A religious ceremony to mark an American Indian child's passage into adulthood.

vigilante Someone who takes the law into their own hands to gain justice for a group of people.

Viking A Scandinavian sea-raider who lived about 1,000 years ago.

war chief An American Indian leader in time of war, usually younger and less experienced than the chief of a tribe.

watch Being on the lookout for danger, or keeping guard.

Wells Fargo Stage-coach company founded in 1852.

Winchester A rifle made by the Winchester Repeating Arms Co., known as 'the rifle that won the West'.

wish book A mail-order catalogue.

wrangler A man or boy who looked after the horses on a ranch or trail drive.

yard The crossbar supporting a sail.

Useful websites

Explorers of the millennium
tqjunior.thinkquest.org/4034

Pirates
www.piratesinfo.com

Pirate legends
www.legends.dm.net/pirates

Pirate image archive
www.ecst.csuchico.edu/~beej/pirates

The Wild West
www.thewildwest.org/index.html

The Oregon Trail
www.isu.edu/~trinmich/Oregontrail.html

The Gold Rush
www.museumca.org/goldrush

Index

A

Abilene (Kansas) 69
Adventure Galley 22-25
Africa 18-20
Alamo, The 47, 49
Alwilda 42
American Indians 46-61, 64, 70, 71, 76
American war with Britain 16, 17
Anderson, 'Bloody Bill' 82
Angria, Kanhoji 42
Anstis, Thomas 38
Apache Indians 58, 86
Apache Kid 82
Arabs 19, 27
Arapaho Indians 54
archaeology 8, 9
artefact, Indian 50-51
assays office 76, 88
Austin, Stephen F. 84
Avery, Henry 28, 38, 42
Aztec Indians 11, 55

B

backstaff 29, 88
Barbarossa brothers 42
Barbary Coast 19
Bart, Jean 42
Bartolomeo 'el Portugués' 13, 42
Bean, Roy 84
Beckwourth, James 'Tomahawk' 49
Bellamy, Sam 8, 9, 42
Benton, Thomas Hart 86
Bierstadt, Albert 51
bilge-water 31, 88
Billy the Kid (William H. Bonney) 82, 86
Black Bart *see* Roberts, Bartholomew

Black Eagle 58
Black Hills of Dakota 76
'Blackbeard' *see* Teach, Edward
Blackfeet Indians 49, 59
blackjack 28
blanket 50, 51, 65
Bodmer, Karl 51
Bonnet, Stede 17, 42
Bonny, Anne 15, 39, 42
booty 36, 88
Borneo 41
boucan 12
Bowie, Jim 49
bowsprit 22, 23, 88
branding (cattle) 62, 63, 88
Brannan, Sam 76
Brasiliano, Roche 13, 42
Brethren of the Coast 12
Bridger, Jim 48
Britain 17, 41
British colony 14-15, 16, 47
bronc-buster 63, 88
Brooke, James 41
Brown, John 82
Brown, Nicholas 42
buccaneer 7, 9, 12-13, 14, 15, 23, 34, 88
Buck, Rufus 82
buckaroo 64
buffalo 52, 53, 54, 56, 88
Buffalo Bill *see* Cody, William
buffalo chip 73, 88
buried treasure 36, 37
Butterfield, John 86

C

Calamity Jane *see* Canary, Martha Jane
'Calico Jack' *see* Rackham, John
campfire song 67
Canary, Martha Jane 86
cannibalism 31, 88
cannon 22, 25, 34-35, 88
capstan 22, 23, 88

caravel 10, 11, 88
careening 21, 88
Caribbean 7, 9, 10, 12-13, 14, 23, 34, 37
Carson, Christopher (Kit) 86
Cartagena 7
cartridge 81, 88
Cassidy, Butch 81
Catlin, George 51
cattle 49, 62-63, 66-67, 69, 71
Cattle Annie 82
cattle baron 63, 88
cattle drive 63, 66-67, 88
caulking 21, 88
ceremony, Indian 59, 60-61
chaps 64, 65, 88
chart 29, 88
Cheng, Madame 42
Cheyenne Indians 58
chief, Indian 53
children 53, 56, 58, 60, 71, 73, 75
Chinese 28, 31, 34, 41, 76, 78
chuck wagon 63, 66, 67, 88
Civil War 47, 82, 88
claim 72, 80, 88
Clanton, Billy and Ike 79
Clark, William 48
Clifford, Barry 9
clothing
  cowboy 64, 65, 68
  Indian 52, 58, 59, 61
  settler 71, 74
Cochise 86
Cody, William 86
coin 37
Colt, Samuel 86
Columbus, Christopher 11, 46
Comanche Indians 58, 59
compass 29, 89
compensation 33, 89
Condent, Christopher 28, 42
Conestoga wagon 71, 89
conquistador 46-47, 89
cooking 57, 67, 73, 77

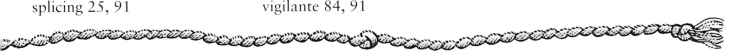

Acknowledgements

The publishers would like to thank the following
illustrators for their contributions to this book:

John Batchelor 22-23, 24; Richard Berridge (Specs Art) 38-39, 41*cr*, 62-63,
64*b*, 65*b*, 66-67, 68-69; Peter Dennis (Linda Rogers Associates) 6-7, 8-9,
18-19, 12*b*, 13*b*, 14*l*, 16-17, 46-47, 48, 49*l*, 70-71, 72-73, 74, 75, 76-77;
Francesca D'Ottavi 30-31, 32, 33*t*, 34-35*b*, 36-37; Richard Draper 9*br*, 21*br*,
28*t*, 29*tr*, 31*br*, 34-35*t*, 36*tr*, 37*cr*; Terry Gabbey (Associated Freelance
Artists Ltd) 52-53, 56-57, 58, 60-61; Luigi Galante (Virgil Pomfret) 78-79;
Nick Harris 4, 5*br*; Christian Hook 29*b*, 80-81, 82*br*, 83, 84*tr*, 85; John
Lawrence (Virgil Pomfret) 13*tr*, 19*bl*, 20*tr*, 25*b*, 86-91; Angus McBride
(Linden Artists) 18-19, 20-21; Malcolm McGregor 49*br*, 50, 56*tr*, 57*tr*,
59*l/m*, 63*b*, 65*m*, 81*br*, 84*bl*; Clare Melinsky 42-45; Nicki Palin 15*b*; Tim
Slade 46-47*t*, 47*br*, 55, 67*tl*, 70*bl*; Peter Thoms 67*br*; Shirley Tourret
(B L Kearley Ltd) 12*tr*, 13*tl*, 14*r*, 15*tr*, 16*tl/br*, 20*bl*, 25*tl/tr*, 33*bl*, 38*bl*,
51*tr/br*, 54, 55*r*, 58-59*t/r*, 63*t*, 64*tr*, 65*tl*, 67*tr*, 72*tl*, 79*m*, 82*l*, 83*b*; Thomas
Trojer 26-27; Richard Willis (Linden Artists) 40-41.

Page symbols (pages 5-41), engravings (pages 46-85) and border rope
(pages 2-3, 6-45, 88-96) by John Lawrence

Decorative border (pages 46-87) by Mark Peppé (B L Kearly Ltd)

The publishers would also like to thank the following for
supplying photographs for this book:

Pages 7, 9, 11, 28, 41: National Maritime Museum; 31, 32: Public Record
Office; 37: Mary Evans Picture Library; 39, 49*r*, 51*tl*, 75*tl*, 79*bl*, 84*br*: Peter
Newark's Pictures – *Fall of the Alamo* Robert Onderdonk (49*r*), *The Cowboy*
Frederic Remington (51*tl*); 50*t*: J. Allan Cash; 57*tl*, 69*tl*: Amon Carter
Museum – *Indian Girls Grinding Corn* Adam R Vroman *(57tl)*, *In Without
Knocking* Charles M Russell (69*tl*); 67*bl*, 73*t*: Corbis/Bettman (UK);
69*br*: Montana Historical Society – *At the Railhead*; 75*tr*: State Historical
Society of North Dakota – *Pendroy Quilting Party*; 77*tr*: Trip/Art Directors.

*Every effort has been made to trace the copyright holders of the photographs.
The publishers apologise for any unavoidable omissions.*